From

The Women's Press Ltd
34 Great Sutton Street, London EC1V 0DX

Maureen Lawrence was born and educated in Leeds, read English Literature at Nottingham University, taught for a while, then went to America, where she studied for an MA at Michigan University, Ann Arbor. It was while in America that she began to write, and was awarded a Major Hopwood Award for Drama. Her first novel, *The Tunnel*, was published in both Britain and the USA in 1969; and *Shadow on the Wall* two years later. Around the same time she adopted two boys, and though she continued to write, published nothing more until 1985, when she was commissioned to write a play for Northern Studio Theatre, then another the following year for Theatre Clwyd (*Black Ice*). Since then she has written two plays for children for Lancaster Theatre, and another play, *The Pergola*, has been touring the Midlands and the North.

She is at present Writer in Residence at Derby Playhouse, and is working on some short stories as well as a sequel to *A Telling and a Keeping*.

Maureen Lawrence

A Telling and a Keeping
A writer's autobiography

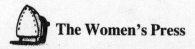 The Women's Press

First published by The Women's Press Limited 1989
A member of the Namara Group
34 Great Sutton Street, London EC1V 0DX

British Library Cataloguing in Publication Data

Lawrence, Maureen
    A telling and a keeping
    1. Great Britain. Social life, 1936–1959.
    Biographies
    I. Title
    941.084'092'4

    ISBN 0-7043-4190-5

Typeset by MC Typeset Limited, Gillingham, Kent
Printed in Great Britain by Cox & Wyman Ltd, Reading, Berks

For Eliza Anne Lyons
born 1875 died 1947

in loving memory

One

Stand still, she tugs, giving the last ringlet a tiny tweak as she twists it round the rag and ties the knot. Pinned between her knees, I stand very still under the open skylight and see a seagull. When she lets me go, I climb on to the bed, stretch out my arms and try to fly. The creaking bed sags in the middle as I jump up and down flapping my wings, until, slotting me between the tight sheets, she says: Lie still now, like a good girl. I lie still like a letter in an envelope, flat and white and paper-thin, listening to her voice going down the stairs. She's a bundle of nerves, she says, like her mother. Her mother's all go.

Is it not good to be all go? My grandmother is a good old fairy. Her black curled cloth coat. Her silver hair. Her gappy smile with a speck on one of the teeth like a tiny tea-leaf. Nobody but me knows she is my good angel. Nobody in the street where we stay for a long time knows my real mother is beautiful. Everybody thinks I belong to a little humped old woman in a black lumpy coat with bunions on her feet and old-fashioned broad shoes that do up with button hooks like a little girl's shoes. I myself long for shoes with laces. I do not want any more ankle straps or cross bars or anything babyish. My grandmother writes to my mother that my old black shoes have fell off my feet. I long for her to come and bring the money so that everybody will see that she is young and beautiful. Her cheeks are soft and pink. She wears a velvet ribbon in her curls. She has tiny feet and white lace gloves that Grandma makes with a hook and thin silk thread. It is called croshering. On the bus back from getting the salads for the high teas, she breaks off a long strand for me to play cat's cradle. You're all go, she says, like your mother, though you feature his side.

At night I lie in the attic, longing for my mother to come and visit me again, but she has sent the shoe-money in an envelope because she cannot afford the fare. The price of shoe leather and it's no better than cardboard, they say, but nothing is the same with the shortages. I make a tent out of the sheet because ever since the trunk was slit I am afraid up in the attic. It is such a long way down to the clatter and help of the downstairs. They are out of earshot unless I make a loud hullabaloo. Then my grandmother will come gasping up the stairs, but I cannot grasp it and give it to her in one piece, the terror that slips out of reach as she enters the door, soothing: Be a good girl for Grandma and lie still. Grandma is coming to bed soon. Soon? Soon as the potatoes is done for the dinners tomorrow. We mustn't make a noise to annoy the visitors. Tell me about the trunk again? Never mind trunk. Is it empty? She lifts the lid to show me there is nothing inside and it opens lop-sided because one hinge has been forced and the leather slashed half-way along and mended with a limp piece of black oil-cloth. Who did it? I whisper. Nobody knows. It was found wrong after the soldiers left last winter. Do soldiers get holidays at the seaside like other people then? Leave, they get. Then she adds: But these poor lads – waiting for embarkation – were billeted here in the off-season when we went home. Have they gone now? Aye. How to form the fearful question without inviting the terrible terror? Are they ever coming back? Let's hope to God they are – for their mothers' sakes. Here? Nay, lass, back to their own homes. Go to sleep now and then Grandma will be up soon.

Peace ebbs with her footsteps, as she falters down the steep, twisting stairs. She is old. I make a tent. There is nobody but me in the attic. But the soldier with his knife has left his imprint in the air. I have forgotten to ask her the main question: Was he one of ours? Ours were heroes. Like my father. But how could one of the heroes steal up the narrow silent stairs and with his pointed blade stab and tear until a long rip appeared in the old trunk in which all our belongings had come from home? He was a thief. A thief as well as a soldier. Grandma laughed: He got nothing for his pains except my second-best stays and a bottle of mentholated oil for rubbing rheumatics. Her stays are greyish pink and floppy with much washing. She holds on to the bed-end while I pull the strings and practise tying bows; the tightening makes her bosoms rise like dough in a bowl on the hearth, but instead of the smell of new bread her skin exhales a special spiciness – camphor in a little flannel bag and, strangely, toilet water. She chuckles at my puzzled face and lets me sniff the little silvery lid of the bottle, and its

2

ticklish scent makes me sneeze. But now the trunk is empty. When I fold down the sheet and lift my head from the pillow I can still see it standing, up-ended, big enough surely to hide a crooked man. There is a crooked silver threepenny bit in the money-box at home . But what is a crooked mile? A crooked mile, smiles Grandma, goes all round the houses and back again. Smile, mile, smile, mile, smile. Smilemilesmile, milesmilesmile. Milesmilemilesmilemilesmile. Miles and miles and miles. Smile, please, says the man on the pier, putting his head under the black cloth. But it would be dark inside the trunk and a crooked man would suffocate or dry up like a spider trapped inside a box. I open my eyes to make sure there are no living spiders, forcing myself to glance quickly into the shadows of the eaves and to wait patiently for her, without crying out and bothering the visitors, because when she comes into the bed in her warm white gown, when her big soft bulk presses the flocks down at her side, so that I roll down the white sleepy slope into the fug of camphor and lavender that is her very own smell, then – oh then – I will be safe.

My mother is an exiled queen. My father is a hero. They are both almost strangers, remote and beautiful. My guardian angel is a little good old woman, who cleans and cooks in a boarding house, where visitors come for their holidays. The people of the house keep us and feed us free instead of giving Grandma any wages, and for everything else she has her pension – for ice-creams and apples and pennies to go on the pier. The man of the house – the mester – grumbles that for me life is one holiday, and if I am a good girl and do not natter Grandma, he gives me a threepenny bit to stay out in the streets, while she does her work. In the kitchen it is very steamy on wet days, when – at a corner of the table on the oil-cloth – I learn my letters on brown paper bags that my grandmother saves and irons for me to use; and all the while they run backwards and forwards with platefuls of food for the visitors, breakfasts and dinners and high teas. I shall have to bring the little lass with me, says grandmother, on the day trip, making the arrangements, but she's not a bit of bother: she'll lie with me in my bed and she eats nothing. Living up to her word at a corner of the kitchen table I take very small mouthfuls so that they will see she was telling the truth, picking out the flakes of dark cabbage from gravy on which float thin floes of congealing fat. In a lull between servings the man looks down at me: he is white and thin and limp as if the heat and steam have taken all the stiffening out of him, so that his lank black hair hangs round his bony forehead in loosely matted loops. Because he has had consumption, he has not been taken for a soldier. He slides the threepenny bit from the top pocket of his white overall, teasing. Outside, he says, when you've licked that plate clean to save your granny a bit of washing up. Outside, says his wife, taking the yard broom from the back porch, pretending to sweep me into the front hall, while at the sink my grandmother stands, not looking my way, not telling me what to do, her wrinkled arms deep in hot suds, her head bowed, not telling me what to do.

Outside I sit on the doorstep for a long time. Across the top of the street there is a windowless wall that looks like a dead-end, until close-up you can see a narrow ginnel that runs between the gable end of the terrace and the blank back-side of a picture house. That is the way other older children of the street go to school. But at the bottom end is a big road across which lies the promenade, the tram-track, the sea-wall and – tide willing – the beach. Beyond, always, mysteriously, the shuttling sea, now near and deep and noisy, now far away and silent in the distance, shimmering, with shallow lapping edges, but always, at its furthest horizon, vast and strange. That way my grandmother is in the habit of taking me every day during her free afternoons, past the ice-cream parlour on the street corner, where I can spend my money, then down the ramp on to the shifting sands. It is nearly time for our outing. I look longingly into the house, down the hall. The kitchen door is slightly ajar. A subdued polite chatter comes from the dining room where they are having apple pie and custard for dinner on their best behaviour. My own pudding is cooling on the side of the sink but they have shooed me out of doors, forgetting to let me finish eating, and I dare not ask for my dish. Perhaps, unwittingly, I was fidgeting, interfering with their work, being a nuisance? Perhaps my foot had been kicking the table leg without my telling it what to do? I look at my feet curiously, dingily clad in the worn black shoes with the bar over the instep and the buttons protruding like the two beady little eyes on shrimps. Like two little animals. Do they have a life of their own? I make my hands into two red crabs that creep down my legs on leggy fingers to nibble my shoes. The toe-caps are scuffed grey. Are they sad and ashamed to be so old? Underneath, the middle of one sole is quite worn through, so that when I walk I can feel the pavement, first of all tickling the underside of my foot and then beginning to burn with friction. There is a blister there under my big toe, and when it

4

burst water came out and the skin went flabby like an empty balloon and then it rubbed broken just like a bit of curled rubber and the skin inside was a clear bright pink the colour of raspberry vinegar on ice-cream in the little glass dishes in the ice-cream parlour window; and a grain or two of sand sneaking under the flap of skin made it sting so that I could not balance any more on my one leg while she shook out my socks, but fell over crying and she took the sore place in her mouth and licked it clean with her warm wet tongue, spitting in the sand afterwards because it tasted salty.

Inside, all along the hallway at the edge of the linoleum, there is sand tracked in by feet. When the woman – only woman is not a polite word, I must say lady – when the lady of the house wafted me on to the front step, she swept the floor too with the stiff brush, just as she did several times a day with the soft brush, knocking the broom head briskly against the skirting board, until at the threshold she gave a swift lift and some of the sand fell over and down the steps in a flurry. Everywhere there is sand – even in drawers and pockets and ear-holes. I pat the steps and feel it gritty under my fingers. When I go to the toilet – which Grandma sometimes calls the closet and sometimes the lavatory – she tells me to wipe and look and wipe and look until the paper is clean, and there are even little bits of grit there too in the crack at the top of my legs. Sometimes she stands me in the sink and slops water up me and calls it my little bit of meat, and when she pulls the plug out of the gaping drain there are skeins of sand on the sink-pot too that she carefully swills away by running the tap till it is all clean. Thinking this makes me want to go. I long to sneak up the stairs and sit on the wooden seat and let myself go. Waiting gives me a pain. How long have I been waiting on the step? I want to call my grandmother but I am afraid the mester might take back the money he has given to keep me quiet. I want to be on the beach. I want my pudding. My pudding must be lonely, waiting. But it cannot be a long time because inside I can still hear the tinkling irregular music of spoons on plates and water splashing from jug to tumbler and voices stifled with politeness. The visitors are all good – like company for tea on Sunday afternoons when the best cups come out of the china cabinet to match the best cloth with the chain-stitch lady who stands on a corner of crazy paving. In the kitchen they will be sitting down at last and eating their own dinner and they will not want to be bolting their food and getting heartburn. Or they will be filling the cups with tea for afterwards out of

5

the big tin tea-pot that is so heavy it needs two handles. Yes, in every house all along the street in all the front rooms the visitors are drinking tea. That is why it is suddenly so quiet in the street in the sunshine, so quiet you can almost believe a spell has been cast and everything has to keep quite still until it is allowed to move again. That is why my bottom has gone numb, because I am turning to stone like the angel statues in the cemetery at home, white and smooth and cold with blank eyes staring sadly holding a stone book with pages that do not turn. And everybody will be sorry because when I was alive I was only a little child.

Rubbing my back-side I shift from the steps to the short slatted seat jammed into the wedge of space between the doorway and the bay window, so that a plank nailed along the jutting window-sill makes a back-rest for grown people. I kneel with my chin on this ledge, my nose pressed against the glass, trying to peep through the lace curtains to make out whether they have nearly finished, hoping that my grandmother will see me if she is clearing the tables and will let me help – first the dirty bowls and the spoons and the cups and saucers, then the cruets and sauce bottles to stand on the piano top, and last of all, heavily, slowly, the big water jugs with the water slops from all the tumblers, before she takes from the mantelpiece the little silky brush and the tidy, whose matching handles are a silver man and his silver wife in olden dress, he with a top hat, she with a poke bonnet, to go flick, flick and smooth away every last crumb from the damask table-cloths. But not until they are done eating. Not until she has finished reaching the hot dripping plates into the wooden rack above the sink, so that the sunlight coming in at the back window winks on the soap bubbles and on the big black stove where the cooking fire will be expiring in a mass of hot white ash.

Tired of waiting, I duck down from the seat and creep round the house on all fours. At the side there is a divide in the terrace, just wide enough for the coal to be delivered and dustbin-men to get the bins, with a high yard wall in which the door is sometimes left unbolted; it has vertical boards that have shrunk with age leaving slits of light and knots that make good peep-holes. I rattle the handle in vain, squinting through the gaps to see what I can see, but there is only a view of the yard with its steaming drain full of suds, its cracked concrete and the dank footings of the kitchen wall. My grandmother is out of sight. The house next door has a hedge instead of a wall, a hedge growing behind a ledge three bricks deep, which makes another convenient seat, where I often squat, waiting. I sit down, pressing my shoulders into the hedge so that the twigs prickle my bare arms. There are some spiky little flowers – the colour of vanilla ice at the end of some of the twigs, and once I found a ladybird that I talked to for a long time until it startled me by unfolding wings out of its red enamelled casing and whirring away out of reach.

But this day there is a boy in the back alley-way. He is smaller than me and is propelling himself along the ground on a little bogey using his hands as levers. When he falls off, I see that his bogey is only a slate tied to a roller skate with a bit of clothes-line. He lies, sprawling, tears spouting at his eyes, until I tell him that nobody can hear him because they have all gone to sleep for a hundred years, and then he scrambles to his feet, weighing me up to see whether I am telling the truth and what I will do next. He belongs to the house next door but we have never played together. He is dirty and there is a thick greenish stuff in his nostrils, not wet but almost solid and crusted round the edges. I am clean. I have a handkerchief. My white dress is starched. It is printed with bows in sweet-pea colours – violet and pink – and it has a wide sash. I am not to get dirty or to toss my head about because my ringlets will get spoilt, ringlets that come out of rags each morning when the lugs make me cry. She looks as pretty as a picture, says the lady of the house. A proper little princess, says the man, rubbing his chin on my cheek and calling it chin pie. And sometimes the visitors take me out with them on trips because I am presentable and know how to mind myself. But the boy is wearing a knitted jersey, very loose and baggy, and short flannel trousers, the kind that all boys wear all the time, only his are soiled and shiny with age, of a mid-grey colour that merges into the grey pallor of the alley-way. The back of the house is not all jolly like the front. Perhaps only the front walls of the houses are painted, to make them look cheerful for the visitors – white and pale blue and pearly pink, sad, faded colours indeed on dull days, but when the sun shines a curious dappled shimmer makes the street seem festive and beckoning, every window lacy with looped curtains and bold signs NO VACANCIES NO VACANCIES and people with suitcases and children with clanking buckets arriving eagerly at doorsteps. And even, now and then, a taxi ticking and voices greeting. But today, in the alley-way, it is deathly quiet so that the possibility of bewitchment seems very real and the boy slips unresistingly into this suspended moment. Together,

7

we perch on the low wall, our backs pressed into the dusty privet hedge, our voices the only sounds, dropping into the vague stillness and loneliness of the afternoon.

This moment is clear, implacably unalterable. And yet, as always, this clarity, this fixity, fills me with profound disquiet. No erasure is possible. I have a sense of things fore-ordained, prefigured in the existing universe. I see the little girl sitting on the cement-pasted wall and the boy rooting in a crumpled paper bag. I catch the faint scented whiff of dolly mixtures. On my palm his fingers place a tiny tablet, powdery, mauve-coloured, heart-shaped; and later out of the shadowy evening in the back-yard a voice will say: She has got a sweetheart, her own little sweetheart. And I will forever connect up the idea of being chosen and cherished with the heart-shaped symbol, the pallid offering sucked lingeringly on that distant yet distinct afternoon.

Yet I was already in love, with a boy and a girl, the brother and the sister that belonged to the people who kept the public house at the other corner: in love with their red cheeks, their shocks of glossy hair, their abrupt unconsidering friendliness, passionately in love above all with their enchanted togetherness. Remember the rapture of being chosen by them to play in the big kitchen above the public rooms. Or of slipping with them into the chocolate-painted porch, where the gleaming skin over the bumpy stucco was pitted here and pimply there with chalky specks; of plunging for one smoky, hesitating instant into the forbidden territory of the bar, the tangle of bodies and uniforms and foam-topped tumblers and tall, round stools, and then up the steep back stairs into their world, where under a great long table we huddle into our secret den; but only for a moment marking out our own space before we begin the fabulous process of construction, building trenches out of buffets and chairs, draping cloths over barricades of step-ladders and ironing boards, their boldness raiding cupboards unchidden to find blankets, biscuits, gas masks, our three beings fused in a hot, busy ferment of engrossment.

It was the war. We built camps, dug-outs, watch towers, look-out posts. We waited with bated breath for the foreign agent, who might be any passing stranger. Each time our fortifications seemed complete, some fresh threat produced a new modification. In this process we were melded together, joined, adapting ourselves instinctively to the moment, while at the same time things lent themselves to us, assuming whatever shape or use we chose according to our needs. Mostly, my

8

grandmother's duties dictated the shape of my days, but these twins provided a further dimension, an example of blissful comradeship that remained for the most part tantalisingly elusive, arbitrary, depending from their intermittent largesse, lapsing between whiles almost beyond memory and hope except as a delicious sense of excitement tinged with danger.

Mostly, afternoons on the beach, we are alone, she and I, she in a deck-chair, wrapped warmly in her old black coat though it is always summer. She calls the coat astrakhan, but I cannot tell whether it is cloth or skin, so tightly curled are its black, furry coils. Her lap is wide, and the photograph, snapped on the pier by a lavish visitor, reveals that standing she is bow-legged. On the sands she slips off her black shoes and softly massages her bunions; and her feet in their thick toffee-coloured stockings are so different from my own thin, flexible extremities that they are more like knobbly old furniture, knuckly chair legs, the stumpy feet of the old sofa at home on which she nurses me to sleep on winter afternoons. Everything that streams out from her to me is absolute – her authority, her love. When she says it is time to go, all my play is rendered null. She grasps me firmly by the elbow, steadying me so that she can flap at my damp, sand-coated feet with my crumpled white socks, tutting. Regretfully I glance down at the mounds of sand, the half-finished ornamentation of the castle-keep – a line of shells, a garland of bladder-wrack, bottle-tops in jewelled colours, ruby and sapphire and emerald – but they are out of bounds, beyond the pale of her permission: it is time to go. In some mute way I understand that her power is benign – and limited. She does not wish to spoil my project, but her free time is gone and she has to return to the boarding-house to wash the lettuce for the high teas and trim off a little border of white fat from the translucent slices of pink ham. Hand in hand we tramp across the soft, dry sand, shoes filling with silt. Behind us the retreating tide has dumped successive bands of glittering treasure. I lag, looking longingly back, tormented by the spirit of quest, till the arc of our arms is strained and she gives a tiny tug. But she does not dawdle; head lowered, she trudges up the sea stairs, and, panting lightly, leans momentarily on the sea-wall. I understand that she is old and that her word is law. Trotting beside her, I lapse into the rhythm of her walk, her breathing, her silent reverie.

One day when the twins came for me, the pub was full of American soldiers. We did not go straight up the back stairs to the private quarters. Perhaps the father wanted to show off the twins to these strangers. Perhaps we were going to the pictures and the twins went to the till to get money. Behind me the street door was open. Light pooled into the dusky interior, illuminating one bright wedge. A draught stirred the atmosphere which was full of minute swirling specks. Outside the brilliant well of light in the dim turmoil of the room there was a huddle of uniforms round a woman in a chair. I was waiting, holding back, ready to run, half-afraid, puzzled. No one spoke to me. No one told me what to do or where to go. Nothing was clear and yet everything was full of meanings for which I had no words. The impressions were struck upon the field of my senses like tiny explosions. I had seen news reels of bombed buildings: mist, dust, noise, confusion, terror. And afterwards a desperate seeking amongst the wreckage. And sometimes a wild joy of recognition. Behind me the door swung shut, cutting off retreat. Somehow I knew the place was forbidden to children. Its smell was rank, fumy, its air thick, turbulent, vaguely threatening, incalculable. Voices were too loud, gestures too large and sudden. But especially round the woman something was not right. Her face was odd, awry somehow. I had never seen make-up on skin. It must have been a thick paint, a liquid mask that had dried unevenly with tight puckers and creases round the nose and mouth and streaked threadlets beneath the ears, flesh pink all over, with lips of clear bright blood. The uniforms of the men were unusually light and smooth, the voices drawling and nasal, and that was because they were Americans, and the woman in the chair belonged to their company, and yet she was different, with something uncanny in her face, ageless, out of kilter, frightening. I trembled, thinking of the witch, the mad queen with the looking-glass that could reveal secrets: mirror, mirror, on the wall. Then suddenly the chair veered round with a flash of steel as the sunlight bounced off the nearest wheel and I saw that she was only a crippled woman with a hunched back and a stiff face; and in the same moment came the revelation that she was a kind of talisman to these men, a focus for their heroism, a justification and a cause, but also a strange kind of play-mate, a comrade in arms, whom her very infirmity had somehow unsexed and thereby endowed with special powers. One of the men pressed into my palm one of those strips of gum wrapped in silver foil, its overlapped edges pinked in minute zig-zags; and while I shyly scraped at this skin of silver, trying to be invisible, the woman tugged mightily at the wheel and the chair surged

10

round right up to my toes, so that I could have touched the grey woollen blanket that covered her dreadful legs. She smiled into my face with her long curved teeth. And then I fled up the stairs after the twins, and the Yanks had given them a film projector and we watched silent movies that unrolled their stories upon an imperfectly stretched sheet on which a hot iron had left faint brown triangles of scorch.

Time. Always time. On Mothering Sunday this year my mother will be seventy. I choose a card that shows a woman and a girl, picnicking by a lake. The picture – sunshine, blue sparkling water, muslin dresses with sashes of vivid scarlet and cerise, straw bonnets, tea-cups with gold rims, and along the margins of the lake a festive throng – belongs in a lost epoch in an altogether different class to which she, finely wrought, vague, decorous, always aspired, so that her white gloves, her handkerchiefs with delicately perforated and stitched edgings, her cake plates adorned with paper doilies, were all somehow emblematic of that higher life that was both interior – her sensibility, her habit of mind – and also out there, beyond, out of reach. There was always a wistful quality in my mother; and a promise that those meetings which I so craved might actually bring about some kind of magical transformation.

Winters we spent at home. Sometimes my grandmother went to stay with her other children, for at that time she had many still alive. Then it was my mother that took me out afternoons to get fresh air. One day – my father must have been still away in the army, which meant that my mother and I were quite alone – one afternoon of all those walks I remember. Most of the war my mother went to work. When she was at home, mornings were for the house and housework. Evenings she sat on the stairs and sang me to sleep. Perhaps she was lonely, crouched there by the stair rails in the twilight, singing very loudly like a huge caged bird, buffing her nails with the little oval pad out of her manicure set and telling me the ideal shape for nails was the filbert with perfect pale half-moons at the cuticle. Afternoons we strolled into districts that were our near but far superior neighbours, where aspiration took tangible shape in wide roads, and trees and houses set apart from each other in gardens. At gates, between gaps in hedges, glimpsing that other life, my mother whispering: a trellised arch, a border of blue lobelia, a bed of roses. Later years, years and years of Sunday outings, made the route – through the suburbs, past the park gates, into the woods – prosaic and familiar, but there is no getting there in my recollection of that afternoon. Out of nowhere it emerges, luminous and complete: my mother and I standing on a woodland path that climbs a slope, precipitous and wild. Everything is at odd, clutching angles: branches, roots and brambles. The air is bleached with cold white light that is coming through high tree-tops, where rooks are building, but below blackness is captured in thickets that seem impenetrable. My mother's foolish heels sink in the yielding earth. Leaf-mould, she laughs breathlessly, a good smell for good growing like the horse-droppings your grandma runs to scoop up with a spade for fertiliser. I breathe in the sweet, sharp smell of deliquescence and peer at the black, weeping fragments, wanting to ask: why good? But her mind moves too quickly for me to catch as she protests: Look at your splotchy legs. And then with sharp excitement: Look!

Below, down the black incline, a sprinkle of yellow stars. Together, quite fearfully, we slither down the bank. A thong of blackberry lightly whips my smeared leg, drawing blood, but I tumble after my mother, who crouches among the tree roots, stroking the yellow petals, her gloves discarded, her eyes enormous, lost in contemplation. Celandines, she says. The word celandine makes me think of Celanese underwear in salmon pink with ballooning legs. Or coltsfoot, she says, I'm not sure. We shall have to look at the library. We can go to the library and find a picture-book. Or ask the lady. We can make a book out of leaves and flowers. A book of our very own in which we can write the labels. Squatting, I am conscious of a dark liquid seeping up between the welts of my shoes and the new leafage, for the ground is boggy and I already know from somewhere – quick-sand, marsh-land, whirlpool – that it is possible to be sucked under and to disappear for ever into the suffocating earth. And then my mother is helping me to peel down my knickers and warm water is flooding out of my body, losing itself steamily in the leaves, and the scratchiness and strangeness of open air is touching my secret places.

Now she is seventy years old, the age of my grandmother at her death almost, yet to me my grandmother was always an old old woman, whereas my mother remains so young. In spite of a life-time she still seems untouched. To me, she seems like someone who, on the verge of waking, will never really be roused, and who therefore will remain forever startled, vulnerable and yet denied the dream. Especially when I was a child, her presence was both alluring and yet dangerous, as if she was liable to lead us into something veiled, menacing, sinister. There was gold in the wood, but there was also doom. I could sense her fear. Her fear of the gathering dusk those lonely evenings on the stair. Her darting glances down shady footpaths into sunlit glades. Her abrupt bridling as a footfall snapped a twig. So that being alone with her was never an unalloyed joy, as if the two of us alone were exposed in our togetherness to a vague threat. And in my imagination that sense of incompleteness, of painful expectancy, became identified with his absence.

It was the war. Over and over again came that suggestion. The penury of those years. That was the war. The shortages. The splitting of the family. The imminence of death by violence. The dark lonely nights in the black unlit street. That was the war. My mother went to work like a single person. But instead of going back to the factory where she had met my father, she went to be trained as a clerk by the War Office, so that my grandmother took me about with her on her travels – to the seaside and to other cities to visit the family – and thus I gained an impression of a populous and perilous shifting world, to which, none the less, we were connected by strong bonds, strong enough to withstand the breaches of time and distance that the war made in the external structure of our lives. Always it was the war. The war had taken my father away for so long that I scarcely remembered his face. He must have had leave. Perhaps my grandmother took me away so that my father and mother could be alone together. At other times my mother went to the army bases and camps where troops were being trained for overseas. I associate him at that time not with any fleeting memory of a visit, but with the one constant image, a photograph taken in the first weeks of his enlistment, a soldier in an immaculate uniform, gazing at me steadily from the dustless surface of the china cabinet. I associate him not with any actual meeting but with the tenderly spoken allusions by my mother and my grandmother and my aunts for whom he was always: your Daddy. The possessive adjective, the diminutive, the teasing chuckle, the wistful note, the assertion – you are your Daddy's girl – the information repeated *ad infinitum* that I resembled him, the picture of a fair, serious face with widely spaced, candid eyes, the squared shoulders, the resolutely folded arms, all these phenomena encouraged the impression that it was his protection we were lacking and that when he returned, when he had won the war, when he and all my uncles and all his friends and all my cousins that were of grown age returned victorious happy and glorious, our world would be complete.

Now, in that same studio portrait, I detect the faint fervour of his complex anxiety: shyness before the camera, a smile for my mother, a questionable future, the thought of manoeuvres next morning, the sheer physical fear of barricades, of sand-bags and thick mire and barbed wire, the squeamish dislike – in spite of his crammed childhood – of the crowded barrack room, a detestation of the enforced regimentation that was – in reality – different from his factory life only in that it allowed him no hours at home and was committed in the name of war. And then I remember that one day in our kitchen one of the soldiers billeted in our street demonstrated his bayonet. Somebody shouted to me to run quickly and have a look. It was the only real gun that I recall seeing in those years of war, though the streets were full of children cocking sticks and taking aim at imaginary enemies. I was told to sit on the sofa and hold out my arms, and the rifle was carefully lowered on to my knees. I shrank away but somebody told me it was not loaded. It meant nothing to me to say there were no bullets inside the gun since I had no conception of how a gun operated. I only knew that it could kill. I was afraid it was going to explode on my legs. It was heavy and cold and large. Somebody – my youngest aunt – was laughing at me. I remember her green sleeves, diaphanous and silky. Somebody said: Look at the poor kid – she's terrified out of her wits. Then it was standing on its wooden end and a word that was new – the word bayonet – was in the room, and there was suddenly a spike on the end of the gun, a spike that was like a very thin, rigid knife, grey with no shine, grey like an old meat skewer in the kitchen drawer, but not twisted. And my father was angry. Yes, he was there after all. He was very angry. He wanted it out of the house. Out of my house, he said. Take that thing out of my house.

Yes. The photograph is in monochrome. Creamy with age, matt and speckled. Yet I always knew the eyes were blue. Yes. Polarities. Smiling. And anger. He had the power to make the gun go away. The laughter stopped when he thundered and people moved softly and swiftly to keep him sweet. When my grandmother – even my grandmother – called him the mester, it was not like the mester she gave to other men, which was title and courtesy, it was an acknowledgement that she was in his house. Move the clothes-horse from the hearth, she said before the mester comes home. He was not her son, but he called her Ma. The two of them were the boss of everything. The mester and the mester's wife's mother. When he went to the war, then Ma was in charge, but when he came home on leave he was the boss. It was his house. He brought treats in his kit-bag: chocolate bars in purple paper, grapes lapped in soft, silvery shavings of white wood, a Gideon Bible with tissue pages that were edged in blush pink, like daisies sleeping. He arranged outings. When he took my mother to the Empire he left my grandmother in charge of me, and he brought her bottles of stout and he put bets on horses for her at the races. When the silver florins chinked into her lap she said: That's champion. And when she lost, she said: Never mind, lad, it's all in the luck of the game. He treated my grandmother almost like a man, but he treated my mother, her daughter, like a lady. A lady does not drink beer or make bets on races. A lady rubs lanoline into her hands and does not say swear words nor speak in a loud voice. A lady gets given jellied fruits in a box with a galleon on the lid and a satin bow bought with coupons bartered from other soldiers, and scent from France, and pink cami-knickers made of *crêpe de Chine*. When he was angry his eyes turned turquoise blue like the glass beads my mother was given by the lady of the house when she was in service; but she did not like being in a strange house sitting in the cold kitchen on her own learning to do fine sewing, and the lady of the house gave her the beads for a goodbye present and she went to work in the factory as a messenger girl because she was neat and well spoken, and there she met my father; and the beads were beautifully glittering but it was not beautiful when his eyes burned blue, and the bayonet went away then and whispers said it was his house and he paid the rent and had the right.

All three of them, they were all good. Even when there were little arguments they were still good. They never shouted or said bad words or had fights like some people in the street. In some of the houses in our family – on both sides – there was fighting and even dirt, but in our house everything was clean and there was never any fighting. As for me, I had to be a good girl for my grandmother and a good girl for my mother and a good girl for my father most of all, because he was not there and because God was watching and knew everything. Being good was being quiet and not getting fidgety, listening and not butting in, not dirtying or tearing precious clothes, not asking for things, not eating noisily, not wetting knickers, not writing on walls or pulling wallpaper or damaging at all, not saying no, not asking for more, not

15

leaving a saucy plate, not pulling faces, not crying to go out to play, or asking to come indoors, not refusing to go to school, not being afraid of the dark, not calling out at night, not tumbling up the bedding in a shared bed, not wetting the seat with drips or leaving the toilet unflushed, not making rude noises, not scratching, not shouting or wandering out of the street or speaking to strangers, not hankering for the moon.

And yet, for all its prohibitions, something in me does not want to leave that time. It was, for all its fears, a time of trust. For above all being good meant being good to each other. The singleness of this intention, the strength of this feeling, the unquestioned nature of our connection with each other gave a sense of total inviolability to our relations. I never remember not being afraid. But the fear and the danger were elsewhere, with the war, maybe, or in the inscrutable darkness at the centre of the earth, or in the spaces and silences of the night, whilst at the place where we were being together, it was very safe.

There, in the sheltering consciousness of their proximity, it was possible to experience an almost blissful absorption of the reality of things, which remains a touch-stone after all these years. I sit on the doorstep at home on a Sunday morning with a metal colander in my lap, shelling peas, The green roundlets drop with a soft ping, one after the other bouncing and dancing before settling still. I nibble at a juicy peascod, sniffing its vegetable perfume, and watch intently as a tiny white maggot eases its jointed body out of a hole in one of the peas. The colander makes a shadow on my dress, but through the gaps in its curved walls spill little droplets of sunlight which move when I wobble my knees. Inside, my mother and my youngest aunt primp new hair-styles in the kitchen mirror, making shapes and bands out of stocking legs: my mother bunches curls from nape to crown, pressing in small combs with latticed edges. A touch of chestnut, she breathes, a trace of the true auburn. My grandmother grumbles at them both for combing their hair while she is preparing food: the stew is in the oven and she is beating batter in a big old bowl, whose brown glaze is crazy with age. Carefully I set down the peas, and after brushing my skirt and pulling the itchy knicker seams out of my cramped crease – I have been sitting on the step a long time again – I take the maggot and put him sorrowfully in the bin, from under the lid of which exhales a stink of rot and ash. Already I am very fastidious and my nose twitches with automatic disgust. Perhaps somebody calls: Come away from that bin. In any case, I do not need telling. I am a good girl. Constrained to sit very still and make no fuss, I am very quiet and self-contained and – like a mirror – reflective. The afternoon is full of the dinner smells from open doorways, the promise of a walk in the park, the shimmer of summer light, the soft, girlish, decorous laughter of my mother, the calm authority of my grandmother's shushings, the knowledge of my absent father, the resonance only half-heard and not interpreted, until, roused by the frantic come-in, come-in, I look up and see droning high above me in the pale sky the solitary flash of a plane and hear somebody crying it's all right he's one of ours, and everybody coming out of doors and craning their necks and waving in relief, and voices telling it's over really it's all over really and they'll be home soon, the men.

Two

Mothering Sunday. Yesterday a table for nine at the Mansion, Roundhay Park. A very brilliant morning: blue-bright sky, hills dazzling with frost. Opposite me at lunch my mother's sister, Agnes, my godmother, aged seventy-eight, hair once ginger, now pale, almost translucent, a shandy shade not unlike diluted light ale, face round, pug-like, whitish-pink, small nose, small mouth over flawless false teeth, vaguely smiling. I try to chat but her answers are ill-sustained, short-winded, tired; and because she was one of those powerful – and beloved – women of my childhood, next only after my grandmother, this decline is telling. She is manifesting the self-absorption of the dying. Ginny's mother, mother of my dear dead cousin, mother first of that one girl who, ten at my five, fifteen at my ten, never to grow older with me, died in a day, after a single night of stomach cramps, a night spent with me in my shared bed, me and my grandmother, a weekend treat that ended in calamity. Years later I learned to pronounce it aunt, the word for her name, so that instead of my anti-Aggie, she became – grandly – my aunt Agnes, by which time, already rendered solemn by two deaths, her daughter, her husband, three if we count my grandmother, she had become part of the antiquated furniture of my childhood, outgrown, outmoded, always – even in her own generation – almost obstinately old-fashioned. And seeing her again, lifting my glass to her, sharing the toast – Mother's Day – though the event celebrated is actually my own mother's birthday, I am dragged back to that day, that D-Day celebration, that night one year after the end of the war in Europe, but before – was it? – the dropping of the atom bomb. Hazy, all hazy that night of torrential rain in Roundhay Park, where an immense display of fireworks across Waterloo Lake in front of a vast crowd sears the night sky with light –

white and lime-green and acid-yellow, magenta and apricot – magically staining the smoke clouds that first billow and then drift and spread across the rain-pierced water.

At lunch in the restaurant the table-cloths are rose-coloured, deep rose, like blancmange dyed with too much of the cochineal with which, tinting water in old medicine bottles, Ginny and I used to dose each other, nurse and wounded soldier in turn, under the tented clothes-horse in the back-yard. The walls, old-rose, are dotted with hunting prints. Our two old men – father, uncle – josh each other about these horses, but the figures predate their era and now their own racing days have become history. I peer over my shoulder, reminiscent: the sporting gentleman in the nearest picture is wearing a top hat and tails. I mention tic-tac men in white gloves and bookies' runners in chequered clothes; the stretched satin back-pieces of waistcoats with tin straps and small brass buckles and across the fronts, fob-watches with seals of carnelian and jet. Nobody says a word, but my mother gives a gentle, encouraging smile. I remind them of those days at the races, those family picnics on the rough-cut grass next to the curving white rails where the horses thunder past, my grandmother's grey travelling rug littered with cup-cake cases and threads of cress and race-cards with strange-sounding names: Double Trouble, Old Man's Darling, Fallen Angel, Golden Simoon. But the old people do not converse. They make scattered pronouncements which loosely connect to form a comforting web around themselves, while I silently call up great bunches of dandelions wilting, and someone saying lion's teeth, and Ginny giggling why do they call them Wet-the-Bed, and her mother saying very vulgar and striking her a glancing blow across the face, and my grandmother saying the girl never meant any harm, and my aunt retorting: No, and a good box on the ears never did anybody any harm neither. And my father is listening for the announcement on the loudspeaker and then laughing, my mother and father both laughing, he leaping joyously to his feet to collect his winnings, she catching hold of him to snatch off the knotted handkerchief, a makeshift sun hat askew across his forehead, tidied and made decent, before he dashes across the course. Now, through the tall sash window, the lawns and cedars look virtually unchanged, but in my recollection these scenes appear suffused with those other moments, antecedents of which no visible trace remains. This present depends from that past. I smile round the table at these remnants of mine, looking for some hint of recognition, and though each one of them – mother, father, uncle, two aunts, husband, sons – smiles back, nods or murmurs, registering the bond with differing degrees of precision and unease, I guess that my preoccupation with the common past is bothersome to the old ones because, standing now at last on the narrow strand, they know that they must go forward on their own.

And so they carp and bicker about a world that is always retreating, Everywhere, beneath the trees – they are complaining – are indications of dereliction. The cuts in public spending are betrayed in these bedragglements: untrimmed shrubs, unmended paths, scantly swept litter. My youngest aunt's lips purse as she comments on this decay. Widowhood sits on her like a cloud of righteousness; and because my other aunt escaped this condition in a second marriage there is a slight friction of disapproval between these two sisters, even after twenty years. For this reason the second husband always offers his comments mildly, delicately, to avoid offence. He alone panders to my nostalgia, remembering the times when the queue for the trams stretched six abreast on a fine Sunday evening, and half a mile long from the gate to the pavilion above the lake where I recall the firework display in the wet black night, and the huge surge as the crowd shifted its face homeward and heaved itself up the hillside that was churned to a quagmire, and the heat of the June storm, my arms wet with sweat inside the clammy rubber raincoat, myself clinging frantically to the blurred, bulky edges of my grandmother, my aunt, my cousins, those solid, defining presences, whose protection still seemed supreme.

Then, as the queue shuffles along the black driveway under the dripping trees towards the tall columns of the gate, my father springs to life out of the night, waving and shouting, his youngest brother, my youngest aunt's husband, smiling at his arm, two brothers and two sisters bonded together by blood and marriage; and my father is shouting frantically, gleefully, above the noise of the rain and the crowd and the feet crunching on gravel and the clangour of the tram-cars and the rising wind: It's a girl. A girl. Another girl. And somebody is teasing: Now then, lad, cans't tha not get thee a son?

Yes, of course, my mother is in hospital. I have known all along she is not ill. I have read the facts out of the newspaper and out of a little leaflet given to my mother at the clinic. My mother is pregnant. This word, so harsh, so foreign-sounding, so often dealt out with bated breath, sidelong looks, carries with it an aura of gravity, almost of wrong-doing. In spite of explanations it is difficult not to believe – with such a word – that she is not ill or that we are not on the verge of some catastrophe. Yet I know she is only having a baby. My father is still in his uniform. All around us people have heard and everybody is shaking his hand. The rain and the tears mingle, streaming down his face. A feeling of extremity seizes me and I too begin to cry, though I do not understand why. Nothing I have been told has anything to do with these sensations, this laughing and crying and teasing, this wetness and blackness and this fear of falling, this flailing of arms and legs, as people push and the huge bulk of the tram looms in front of us and above us, all lit, till I am half-lifted, half-dragged on to the sodden platform, half-blinded by rain and tears. A sister. My mother's sister, Aggie, dead Ginny's mother, is sobbing, and someone is saying: For every one that is taken another is given. And in a week or two – but I do not know it yet – my sister Angela will be named by my aunt – but not Virginia, not that unlucky name, because Ginny has already died and her death, the first death, has already taught me the first, the most tremendous lesson in life: that there is after all no safety, not even truly in these tribal connections; because out of the night, in a moment, in the sheerest, merest instant of time, it can stop, the heart, so that lifting my head time and time again from the pillow, fighting off sleep in the steamy foldings and pleatings and crumplings of my grand-mother's nightly gown, I will listen now and for ever to check the beating of my own heart: listen listen and again listen.

Appalled at these ravages of time, I glance covertly at my aunt's placid features. In her cupboards there were cherished keepsakes over which I brooded with secret envy: a long prism that could ring the world with rainbows; a tulip-shaped vase of green frosted glass, its petals thickly veined and curled, given by the doctor's wife where she had been a cook; a dinner service that was won by my grandfather for an angling prize with a design by Angelica Kauffmann printed imperfectly on each piece; a red jar with butterfly wings captured beneath the glaze. When she turned out the shelves I could touch these old treasures. She taught me to fold the stiff shelf paper and to cut the edges in scallops, and she gave me the spent gauze of the gas mantles to make a skirt for a peg dolly, and showed me how to knit with wool and how to hem with tiny stitches and how to bend brandy snaps over the handle of a cold spoon, and told me a woman must learn to make a good dinner if nothing else and to let the batter stand for at least three hours in a cool place, and to scour the stove with washing soda and scalding water once a week. And everything was serene in her house, where upstairs to the very top, in the attic room with the staircase making it like a landing, Ginny and I used to talk and giggle and suck fruit gums from a shared tube; and once when I was almost asleep and could hardly hear, a voice so faint and far-away told me – she did – that I should find a little thing between my legs, and me wondering did she mean little like a dwarf or little like a pin, and she fingering – did she? – or perhaps me later after she died, when again I went upstairs to the very top to look at the relics of her little life: the dressing table with the felt rabbit in the peasant frock; the chest in which for a long time her unfinished sewing waited for her to come back and take it upon her lap and put in the final stitches.

Appalled, I wonder whether her mother remembers the things that I recall with such agonised clarity, and whether there is anything to be gained from these old stories. Why should it still matter so much that a girl called Virginia lived for such a short time so long ago in a cobbled street in a house that we called back to back in a row so similar to all the other rows that only we could know the difference? Such belonging. But already, when Ginny died, abruptly, unnecessarily, this rootedness took a great wrench, and compared to this fact of death the facts of life – printed for mass consumption in the little blue booklet, its clinical terms simplified and neutered, whispered in sheds and shelters, shouted from the corners of alien streets, foreign territory guarded by raucous boys, scrawled on the playground wall in stolen chalk – these facts of life seemed utterly mundane. So that sensing the wariness of parents at the sharing of these particularities – eggs, tadpoles, the wriggling of weary urgent multitudes along steep red canals – it was necessary to simulate astonishment: Ah! so this is how it comes, a baby out of these specks, these droplets of seminal fluid, these gradual transformations. Thus, sitting on a kitchen buffet, darning a sock, reading a series of articles on reproduction, my mother, flushed, smiling shyly in a floral smock, my father peeling potatoes on to a discarded sheet of the same paper – the church bells are pealing too that day – while I tried to flatten my bumps of knowledge, wanting them to believe in my innocence, feeding their need to feel needed, feeling already, because of so many counter-indications, that in spite of their admirable frankness there must be something dark and secret in these mysteries of science, something not told.

I sit at a north-facing window, composing myself. The map of the past, of the streets is in my mind, but as the years pass, decay begins to erode and erase even these interior territories – like demolition. Rubble, broken brick, split stone, chunks of mortar, picked clean of lead piping, fancy finials, anything that has become saleable or collectable or both: these spectral landscapes. Devastation. Waste. Waste. My place. My very own beginnings. Sometimes, when I think of Eliot, whom I so loved in my student years, murmuring his lines, his barren land, his lilacs, I am conscious that he has stolen something from me, something he could not own, arrogating to himself those images in which to enshrine his special vision. What could he really know – this privileged alien – of these people? Only I have the key. My sharing puts me inside the man in shirt-sleeves smoking in the alley-way. Thus and thus I stand in the attic, holding the dismembered pieces of the blue dress with its soft velvety nap, trying to bring her back, the sense of her, the look of her, the pale red hair that was thin and fine as floss, the violet eyes, the albino look about the eyes of the true red-head, though then that was only her special face that is unlike the face of any other and is now no longer. My sense of destiny is enormous, ominous. On the pocket, child-like, before the parts are put together, she has already begun to work the embroidery motif, a glittering flower in blue bugle beads: a tissue paper full of skeins of beads slips out of my fingers on to the floor, sneaking under the tongued tufts of the rag rug. Terrified, I fling everything back into the tin trunk and, lest I should conjure back her forbidding ghost – for she was a tyrannical possessor of her own things – I tumble down the cramped winding stairs into the warm safety of the room.

Yet I cannot recover it all. Must it be lost? My memory reaches behind those net curtains into cupboards and drawers, those precious relics, those battered suitcases crammed with documents, births, marriages and deaths in faded copperplate, pressed flowers of papery paleness, those intricate relations. Because it was not at all as they have witnessed, those curious interlopers, making their simple diagrams of the poor: Eliot and Orwell and all the rest. The uncouth resonance of their misheard dialogues misapplied infuriates the practised ear, the knowing heart. When my father got demobbed, he was given a suit of clothes, a raincoat, a Bible and a little money; and because he was a man that worked in the industry and knew cloth and the cut of a good suit and the finish of a tailored make, it was

23

impossible for him ever to wear a set of garments of that kind, a joke suit with no fit and a deadness in the stuff that showed – they said – it had been spun out of the sweepings of a mill floor. But out of his severance pay he bought and carried across the sea those bunches of black grapes with a silvery bloom on their skins, grapes that nestled in scented shavings in a crate strapped round with metal tape; and underneath the fruit, carefully inserted into a thick army sock, was a slim box of coloured pencils – not waxen in their wooden centres like ordinary crayons, but soft and powdery like chalks. From the very beginning, my conception of my father as a force to be reckoned with, an absent power in our midst, was shot through with a sense of his munificence. His return was connected for me with a feeling of heightened potential, an expectation that energy and delight would surge into our lives. The baby that was going to be born would belong to me in a way that the twins – retreating into memory already – and even my cousins could never belong. His presence seemed to validate our existence not merely because he would be strong, but because he was associated with a notion of well-being, with birth and peace, and good food, and rejoicing.

It is Sunday morning and it is winter. No difficulty in finding the exact time because there is a fire in the grate, hoar frost outside on the privet hedge and my pregnant mother is lying in bed late; the winter therefore before the June when my sister will be born. I sit on a stool darning my father's socks. I use a wooden mushroom. The hardness of the wood, the delicate scratching of the needle, the webbing of the wool, all this is pleasant and soothing, almost soporific, so that I feel as if I am in a warm swoon, as good almost as walking to the shops alone, entering the closed yet marvellously expansive space of private thought. Yet there is nothing as definite as thought in these moments. The darning mushroom – bought at some church bazaar and painted gold – has a grainy surface that gleams through the latticework of the darns, warning me when the interweavings are too loose; there is an exquisite pleasure in perfecting these lines and making them form exact parallels. The fire whispers: criss-cross criss-cross criss-cross. It is very quiet in the room. Everything is brown and rust – the rug, the linoleum, the leatherette of the sofa with its let-down arms – and though there are no ornaments or pictures, nothing but articles of use, the kitchen is the cosiest room. My father is reading the Sunday paper: the *News of the World*. Later it will be used for trash and for covering the mat at the door on rainy days, days when, squatting to change my slippers on coming home after school, I will sneak a look at the stories of vile crime, which my father only glances at incuriously before turning to politics and sport, sometimes reading aloud to my mother, who now and then interrupts gently to correct his pronunciation. Kneeling to read in stolen snatches, I mouth the words that are never uttered in these shared readings and feel the shuddering, baffled horror that sometimes assails me when I find myself alone and gives a disturbing authenticity to those vague night fears: necrophiliac, prostitute, homosexual, vice. Out there – I have known this on the pulse for a long time – is a frightening world where villainous beings stalk and, though they have no claws and tails, no iron teeth that rip and tear, they are capable of monstrous cruelty.

But here we are safe. My father has taken breakfast on a tray upstairs to my mother, spoiling her because she is having a baby, and we are alone in the kitchen with the ticking clock and the lingering smell of frying bacon and the streaked plates pushed to the centre of the table. Perhaps – in a moment – he will tell me abruptly to clear the table and wash the pots. I must not need telling twice. Or perhaps he will ask me to read aloud from the paper, and because reading is a pleasure and an act of pride, because I am the best reader in the whole class, I feel a vague sense of happy expectation, partly connected with the ration of sweets that is always fetched on Sunday morning with the paper and doled out to me with teasing injunctions to make them last. There is a certain roly-poly of coconut candy that I will barter for with half a dozen of the ordinary liquorice all-sorts and the thought of its chunkiness and flavour makes my eyes keep straying hopefully to the waiting box.

At last I finish the darn and hold out the sock for him to admire. But he is no longer reading. He stares at me, unseeing, with a stern face. My heart gives a tiny skip. What have I done wrong? I look down in confusion at the brown sock. Perhaps he is playing a joke? His face twists, and suddenly, suddenly his head ducks down, his head and shoulders crashing down on to the newspaper, on to the crusts of scorched toast on the kitchen table. A cup half-full of tea wobbles in its saucer. Mystified, unable to put a name to what is happening, I remain riveted to my seat. He is wearing a loose white undervest which has lost its elasticity in many washings and which hangs limply on his large white shoulders. His arms are freckled and thick and the hair on the crown of his head is scant and grey. I hear a groaning noise, and only then do I realise that my father is sobbing aloud and that his crying is not like the moist whimpering of a child, but is a dry-voiced sound, a roaring and a gasping, because he is struggling to hold back the flood. Men do not cry. Panic-stricken, I let out a wail. If I begin to cry, he must stop. But I cannot cry. I fly to the hall door, meaning to call, but I cannot call. I fling open the bedroom door, the door of the big bedroom where long ago in the boat between their two bodies he used to rock me and sing songs on Sunday mornings, only I cannot mount the stairs and instead I stand very still on the first tread.

After a while my mother comes out on to the landing wearing an old cardigan over her night-gown and carrying her clothes. Shall I be a softie? she smiles. Shall I dress in the warm? I nod. What is your Daddy doing? I shake my head. I begin to cry. Then my mother is in the kitchen. And she is holding him tight, kneeling by his chair to put her face against his head and shushing: There now, it's better now.

Nothing is ever said. Afterwards his face is red-raw around the eyes and nose and he crawls out of the room and goes to put on his best clothes for our Sunday walk. Nothing is ever put into words to me, but I pick up clues: his nerves are bad. It is the war and the things he has witnessed in the field and in the camps. My mother says: Shush. In a little while I will go to brownie camp for the first time. This seems to be good. It puzzles me that camp can be good and bad. My mother says again: Shush. Certain things cannot be shushed. Everybody knows that life is hard and times are bad and that making ends meet is a terrible burden on a decent man. The prospect of coming out is ahead of my father, but the gratuity is needed for the new baby: if the two events do not coincide the baby will lie in a dresser drawer lined with old blankets and my mother will not be able to walk her out unless she can borrow a pram. My mother keeps saying: We'll manage somehow. But my father is not a calculating man – though he is a gambler – and his mettlesome spirit is abraded by these domestic cares. Gradually certain rituals reveal themselves to be economic realities: a larder with a cold stone slab on which every egg is counted; the back of old envelopes on which every penny spent is retrospectively regretted; a tin money-box which never contains more than a few coppers, a silver threepenny bit, a bent florin. No amount of addition sums can really increment their income. His nerves are bad. Soon there will be four of us dependent upon his earnings. My mother's job has already ended with the war, and the factory to which he will return as soon as he is free is working short-time. There is never going to be enough money for our needs.

But he is a skilled workman with a trade at his fingertips, and if his nerves are bad and he cannot earn enough money the fault lies not within him – for he is a good man – but in the system. How already do I know these truths? Nothing is said to me directly of politics, but my father goes to union meetings from which he comes back full of angry assertions, for there is, briefly, at the end of the war, a spirit of resistance in the air, a refusal to take himself, to let them take us, at our monetary valuation. His actual worth is never in question. My grandmother calls him a good lad. If his nerves are bad, if he is no longer the same smiling person that went away, it is because of the camps. In the last months of the war he has been with the forces that guard certain camps. What camps? Hush, in front of the child, says my grandmother. The things that he has seen have crept into his soul and he is not the same man. There is a grim bewilderment in my father that manifests itself to me as rage, the obverse side of his Sunday morning grief, that comes out of nowhere, that strikes where it will, that is entirely authorised because it is his rage, his grief, and that gives him terrible power.

I think forever afterwards when I felt his mood shift towards the negative, my heart would always miss a beat. I think my fear of him took its first definite shape that morning. My mother put her arms around his shoulders. I was shocked by the nakedness of his large white arms. His desolation was a dreadful pit opening in front of my eyes. A pit of bones. Soon it would close over and he would move on to some new place in his experience, ostensibly forgetting or accepting the death chambers except perhaps in the dark night of the soul. But I would always remember and be afraid that some minimal gesture on my part might produce an unaccountable recoil. And so I discovered that I felt at fault in his eyes. And as I grew, I came unwittingly to seek his approval, not because I valued his esteem, but because I was afraid of his demons. To placate, to conciliate, to disarm, to be as quiet, as inoffensive, as proper as possible in his eyes became all my aim. And whatever was not, according to his rule, the correct behaviour I schooled myself to suppress or conceal, not advisedly but involuntarily, out of the same fear that makes a startled spider cling motionless to a wall.

Maybe it was otherwise. The constant search for approbation. For years I believed this was my particular neurosis. Now I tell myself: it was a general state. We were made that way. Because, after all, even when I was contentedly darning the hole, bringing home my top marks, smiling up at the headmaster as he patted my curls and praised my rendition, heaving my gorge as I forced myself to swallow the cold black cabbage, I was already looking for rewards. Thus, there was no moment of trauma: only instances when something out of the ordinary – father crying – revealed the ordinary. What I see now is that though he had so much power, though his word was law, though I would no sooner have thought of denying him than I would of cutting my own throat, he was always vulnerable. I nearly said weak, but that would be wrong because it has pejorative overtones. I do not mean weak in a moral sense. I mean simply that he was subject to the pressures and evils of a system that used him evilly as first factory, then army fodder, and again to the factory, used him for fifty years of his active life. And in the bits of his time and mind that were not usable he was forced to fettle for himself, to make ends meet and to protect his own position and his family. And the hardship of it all, the back-breaking, mind-binding grind of his life, was put upon me as a reason why I should obey him and struggle to escape upwards, up the invisible ladder. It was for his sake that I had to be good girl, but my obedience was not founded upon any conscious reason. It was as if his will belonged to being as air belongs to breathing; like air it filled all the space. Life was inconceivable outside this medium. And just as he was subject to all these inimical conditions, so we – daughter, mother, sister, even grandmother – were subject to his will.

Or else. But no alternative exists. One cannot utter the inconceivable; it is uncreated. To think of putting oneself outside the pale of his permission is to imagine entering into chaos. Terror at the thought curtailed thought. I passed from a magical to a factual conception of the moral universe without at the time being aware of making such a transition, because there was a remarkable consonance between the two phases. Thus, in the earliest of tales – at first not read but whispered in the lap by the fireside when my grandmother crunched bits of butterscotch, passing them from her mouth to mine, and later heard over and over again in school – I had learned that to follow the golden rule of obedience was to arrive safely out of the wilderness and claim the prize – the prince and the promised land. In the realm of disobedience, monsters lurked, with their iron teeth.

But at this time I began regularly to read the newspapers – kneeling on the prickly mat at the door – to read stories of girls who simply disappeared into this black void to be found weeks later, perhaps dead or mutilated or, worse still, transformed into wicked inhabitants of those nether regions by creatures of even greater depravity than themselves. And at the same time – in church, which we had irregularly attended during the war – the words became familiar, ceased to be a soothing mumble and began to form repeated patterns of meaning, amongst which one central motif was dominant: namely the idea that each finite soul is capable of infinite possibilities. Good and evil were human attributes, but their existence was never in question. So that by some process of association the fear of displeasing my father was not a fear of inducing some minor domestic explosion, it was a fear of disrupting the moral order and thus bringing about my own destruction.

My father was an excitable but outwardly mild man, who rarely shouted and never used force; yet after the years of women's voices – mother, grandmother, aunts, cousins – his seemed stentorian. This loud voice at the door, the very thought of causing him displeasure, was enough to set my heart thudding. A feeling of oppression became indentified with his mere presence in the house. His eyes were very blue. When he was studying the newspaper, reading aloud in his halting voice, or engaged in any effort of concentration, even an animated conversation – and he was always talking – the eyeballs seemed to bulge slightly so that the blue blazed with an extra frightening lustre. From time to time someone would say: She's got her father's eyes. Then I would stare at my face in the mirror until the eyes became unreal, rounded like two glass marbles, but full of mysterious opacities, glossy, exterior, yet strangely connected to my own interior self. This close scrutiny revealed a kind of bizarre substantiality that seemed ugly. It bred a kind of terror. I wanted to resemble my mother. It seemed somehow shameful to be like this man, shameful simply because he was a man, not because he was unprepossessing in any way. On the contrary, he was generally regarded as a handsome man; he had a kind of unassuming charisma that was recognisable in some of the screen stars of those days. It was just that the fear he inspired was very like the night-terrors, as if the something that lurked in lonely and dark places became embodied in his person, lying in wait there until I made some accidental error, when it would be unleashed in all its fury. And if in actuality this never happened, it was only – it seemed –

because I was a good girl. I never dreamed of giving trouble. Clever at school, helpful in the house, courteous to teachers and family, quiet at play, docile at work, anxious to please at all times, I kept myself up to the mark and fretted at the slightest fault. Time and time again he questioned me about my lessons. And though in the early days I was generally top girl and was often praised by other people, I never really believed that I had succeeded in pleasing him or meeting with his approval. And thus, however happy and successful I seemed to be, at the centre of myself – on the other side of those impenetrable eyes – I was always conscious of a lack.

Now his word was law and my grandmother was superseded. In the summer that my sister was born my grandmother more and more began to go away on visits without me. My mother came home from the hospital in a taxi and I was allowed to carry the baby on my lap. My grandmother was there at the gate that day to see the baby in its pale pink shawl, but soon afterwards she went away again. Preoccupied by this new arrival I scarcely noticed the other changes and thus, imperceptibly, I passed from the orbit of my grandmother into his demesne. Once home at last, he was there not as the bringer of treats and outings, but as the central pillar. The war was over, and with it the sense of anticipation, the looked-for peace, the bliss of peace to come was gone. For peace was only the absence of war. A kind of lapsing into endlessness.

On this festive day, this Mothering Sunday, even now, thirty years or more since I first left home, seeing them both side by side – mother, father arm in arm, he unsteadily, his joints arthritic, she a decade younger, lithe, unencumbered by disease, her blue eyes gazing back at the Mansion, softened by sentiment, remembering her dead, her eyes full of that perennial sense of the drama of her existence that is her gift to me, supporting him across the car park, a smear of gravy on his chin, his cheeks flushed with wine, his cresset of white hair fluttering in the wind, intent on escaping out of the cold, seeing nothing outside the ambit of his own urgent needs, his bladder, his weak tea, his hatred of draughts, his warm bed – I still ask myself: Am I doing it right? I see them settled into their bungalow and leave them guiltily, evading my mother's unspoken plea for an early visit. She dare not let him hear her ask. I find myself marvelling that his erstwhile dominion has lasted so long. She still conciliates; I still defer. We are still keeping the peace. Only now I do by choice and policy what then I did out of necessity.

Once I stopped expecting my mother to be mothering, we became allies. Very gradually I realised that she would always be younger than me. And thus from the time we were both orphaned by my grandmother's death until I was in my mid-teens, during five years or more, we became united in a tacit conspiracy to help each other and to enjoy ourselves in spite of my father, though it would have surprised us both, and deeply shocked my mother, to hear such a charge.

I am a little mother, smiling and proud. It is dim in the back of the taxi on the slippery dark red seats. The baby is wrapped in a pink shawl – very pale – its intricate weave is a multitude of tiny interlocking loops. The face of the baby is dark pink, somewhat wrinkled, with tightly closed eyes. One very small hand protrudes. The fingers are fully formed but unbelievably small and cool. Pinch very gently, says my aunt, and feel how the bones are like rubber. See the pulse throbbing in the forehead where the skull is not yet sealed. My mother is wearing a loose brown coat the colour of dried blood, which makes her look very tired and plain. I am nearly ten years old. The baby is sleeping. What colour are the eyes? All babies have blue eyes, my aunt replies. Once or twice the eyes flicker open and they are not blue, but neither are they brown – nor grey – nor green. They are dark and cloudy and purplish. Unfathomable. I am elated, holding the baby, but the mood in the taxi is muted and this seems puzzling, until I realise that both women are watching the money-meter and counting the cost. Instead of being transported by this experience into the blissful condition of belonging, I feel curiously aloof and alert, seeing everything sharp and clear even though it is dim in the back of the taxi on the slippery dark red seats, where the baby on my knee is swathed in a very pale pink shawl.

It was a game at first. At the very beginning the game simply sprang into play like matchlight suddenly flickering to illumine a single image in the darkness: two or three pieces of flame-coloured silk on a dusty, wine-red rug, or a new crust chewed to warm pulp in a baby's wet fist. Little by little it became more elaborate, more deliberate. Now I know it was a naming game, but then it had no name. Crouched at the edge of the sea, ankle-deep in sea-litter, I am transferring bits of shell, bottle-tops, shards from the wet, ridged ground into my wet pockets, and nothing is allowed a place without its label: striped, stippled, sticky, purple, pearl, pale, peeled stick, brick, black blade. Before long these items will be discarded, yet they will retain a mysterious permanence that is deeply satisfying, because I am the keeper: they have been imprisoned in my brain and can be summoned at will. Moreover, they are entirely at my disposal. In one of the cells I might keep shells, in another pebbles. But some other time I might make a different sorting. And that also would become true. For everything that was out there could be brought inside here, subjected to the same ordering. And because the everything was so immense and so multifarious, there was an inexhaustible supply of material; till at length it became apparent that to play the game was to accept a challenge. There was an underlying principle, an assumption that it was possible and necessary to be both accurate and complete in the listing. The need to achieve completeness gave a forward thrust, an urgency to the game, but the desire to get it right acted like a brake. Caught in this tension, intent, it was as if an arbiter inside my head would reject every incorrect connection. As if somewhere inside myself, part of me could always be trusted to get it right.

This is the crux of the matter. Somewhere – whatever the prohibitions – there was a kind of freedom, a place where I was the best judge. This good place was inside my own head. But the walls of this place were strangely unstable, because being was becoming, a process of accumulating and shaping that was begun and continued there in the head, in the world where subject and object meet and merge to make a person. Now, as I gazed down at the baby's eyes, my vision contracted to a pinprick of light and my judgement became concentrated into one enormous question. Can the baby see me? The baby is blind, said my aunt, the baby cannot see. Because being was becoming. But at that time I did not know that I myself was still in the making. At the time I was only a good little mother with the baby on my knees and the taxi jolting up the cobbled back street and my grandmother standing at the gate.

Three

My grandmother wanted to die at home. She had been staying in the country with a daughter that had gone into service long ago and had ended up as housekeeper to the vicar. An uncle that was a driver for the corporation managed to get hold of a car and we went to fetch her back on a limpid day in early autumn. The village was in a valley in the fells, full of stone cottages and mills; that day a pall of smoke from the coal fires and furnaces and tall chimneys lay in the still air like a thin grey veil. In the war I had played spies in those hills with cousins and hiding from the enemy, had watched streamlets weeping out of the walls that were furred with brilliant green ferns, while my grandmother had spread her waterproof on the ground and shared out beetroot sandwiches and gingerbread. My aunt lived in a cottage called East View. Each morning it had been a treat to look out of the bedroom window and see wide open spaces instead of streets. And once, stranded above the moor-tops like a huge, silvery sky-whale, there had been a barrage balloon. She's in bed, my aunt said, shaking her head. Unwittingly, I rushed up the stairs ahead of my mother and into the room. And then I stopped, terrified to find that she had become unrecognisable: transformed by a cancer that had given her jaundice, my grandmother was yellow and gaunt, Unable to go forward, I stood in the doorway trying not to look at her face, until my mother reproachfully told me I could go and I went out of the front door which gave on to a field and watched some red hens fussing round a pan of grain.

On the way home she gave me shelled walnuts in a brown paper bag and the car had to be stopped to let us both be sick. My mother tenderly wiped her mouth with a rag that was stained with strands of green bile like the duck-droppings on the park path where once when I fell she had cleaned my mucky knees with her clean handkerchief and a ball of her own clean spit. Now, a bed was set up in the sitting room and a fire was kept alight all the time. For a month or two relations were constantly coming and going. People brought flowers and fruit and fruit cordial and coal and news, and because she was in pain and heavily drugged she hardly talked at all, just smiled and closed her eyes, willing herself to die. At last she did die, and there was a big funeral with seven cars following the hearse and the street lined with neighbours, and me walking behind with the baby and some little cousins. Pushing the pram to the cemetery, where we had often gone together when she was alive, I looked at the raw place with the heap of flowers; but whereas I had once wondered whether the name of the ache I felt for my cousin Ginny was grief, I found myself unable to feel for my grandmother. Ginny's death had forewarned me and I had made myself numb. Something in me had died or grown defective. There is a darkness in those winter days as if I am remembering in monochrome – the black earth, the white flowers – so that even when I see the colours of things, the great waxen chrysanthemums with bronzed petals like cat's claws, the ink on the cards, blotched and moistened by mist, the things themselves lack luminescence, as if something in my vision has gone wrong, causing me to see everything in bleak light: there was an ugliness in the world that no amount of goodness could ever redeem. I did not grieve for my grandmother; I grieved for my own desolation.

In the sitting room, with its coverings of brown moquette and its china cabinet with a lace runner and an untouchable glass basket of fruit, on mild wet days I am allowed to sit and read. A photograph of my grandmother sits on the cabinet opposite my father, but there are no other ornaments, no pictures, or books, no clutter of any kind. There is a carpet on the floor and wallpaper on the walls, with a faint, oatmealy grain. It is very sad in the room. At first the rain pricks the glass with stars, and after a while streams down the windows, blurring the street where the smooth, purplish-red brick of the walls, washed and refreshed, has a leaden gleam. My grandmother's white coun-tenance smiles on at me impassively, and even when I take hold of the photograph and hold her to my cheek, trying to force a connection, she does not change. My mother asks me what I think I am doing, and I stare dumbly, seeking sympathy, but she tells me not to be so silly. At once I realise both that it was her attention I was trying to attract by taking up the photograph, and also that she has entirely missed the point. We have never shared more than the briefest and most intense moments of intimacy. But ever since my earliest childhood I have looked upon her as I once looked upon Ginny, as a limb of myself; with the recognition of her failure to understand, I sense myself being pushed off balance into the curious vacuum of the dim brown room, the wet lonely street. After a while I pick up the book and allow myself to sink into it, to slip gratefully, released from myself, into the blessed oblivion of its pages.

Reading was a refuge. The women in my family were all great readers, but their reading was sporadic and casual; books were not bought and owned, they were borrowed and shared and sometimes, when their contents were questionable, hidden amongst the hats in the wardrobe, or forbidden altogether – like the scandal stories in the Sunday paper. Reading good books was a permitted exercise of the will and a virtue, but it was possible to possess a surfeit of righteousness, for reading could make a person reclusive. Such a person would become a book-worm. The very word conjured an image of something white and burrowing and blind. My own eye-sight was weak. If I read too long I would be sent out to push the baby to the nearest park. Or I might be given a pair of my father's old work shears and sent out of doors to clip the privet and get some fresh air in my lungs. Or a bit of old clothes-line and told to skip a hundred times for the circulation.

When I surfaced from an engrossing book, the real world seemed alien, full of gaps and imponderables. I sat in the sitting room alone, while the street outside pursued its course: a postman scratching his head as he looks at an envelope; a small boy sailing a match-stick boat down the swollen gutter; two girls playing tipple-tails on an iron-railing; a blind fiddler sheltering in a doorway out of the rain. But whereas at one time such solitude had been a temporary pleasure, it now seemed an absolute and enforced condition, like solitary confinement. Prison stories left me feeling feverish with sympathy. This separateness was not purely mental, for after my grandmother died there was no one to share my room. During her short illness I had slept in the little place we called the box room above the stairs, while my sister's cot was pushed out on to the landing. But one weekend Ginny's mother and her husband, who was my favourite uncle, arrived with buckets and brushes and the old room was emptied of its furniture and then stripped of tired old paper that had been washed over with a yellowish distemper many times, so that the soaking cloths were stained and slimy with pigment and the water in the buckets slopped orange pools on the floor and made tidemarks on my aching arms, as I too scraped the walls. When the room was scrubbed and the bare plaster repainted, everything was put back in its place. Her grave old furniture with its scrolled headboard, its triple mirrors, its pendant handles of cool grey metal, became my furniture, in which certain vestiges of her life remained stored for a little time. There was an astrakhan muff, a Gladstone bag with a broken brass clasp, a small wooden box full of tiny glass beads and a pillow-case that contained a dozen huge rainbow-coloured plumes from an unstitched ostrich feather fan, which disappeared one day as inexplicably as it had first appeared. For a while it seemed irreverent to allude to these grandmotherly things; people looked sad at the least mention, and later nobody except me seemed to recall or wonder about the fan. At first I was afraid even to go into the room or to lie in the bed, where she had died, but when I shrank away my mother reproached me: She loved you best of all.

At night my mother always came to tuck in the sheets and kiss my cheek. Sometimes she used to say wistfully, when he was going out of the house: Kiss your Daddy goodbye. But mostly there was no touching. At a time when washing was a quick wipe in a cold room and the very word body still carrried forbidden connotations, I did not even touch myself, rarely saw myself and did not like what I saw – a pale face with eyes, brown hair with a slight wave scraped back into two thin braids. In my class at the grammar school there would be several girls with beautiful flaxen hair, some with rosy cheeks. one or two with curling eye-lashes, and a few girls with downy skins that looked as if they were bathed every day and patted with soft towels. By and by we talked, in class, a greal deal about these attributes, and there was never the least doubt in my mind that I was one of the plain ordinary girls that made up the inconspicuous majority. I associated this benighted condition with the fact that I resembled my father when, according to all natural expectations, a girl ought to be like her mother.

That summer, before I went to the new school, my father decided to teach me to swim. When I was ten, he was already forty, to my mother's thirty. His superiority in years was augmented by a sense of his confidence and intelligence: he was quick, sharp, and dogmatic –

intolerant of any views that did not coincide with his own. Physically he was neither tall nor large, but he was energetic and the sense of his power was tremendous. It gave him a sort of spiritual bulk, less steady and neutral than my grandmother's, with more in it of animation and impatience. He never threatened or bullied, never participated much in things of the house, was either at work or out in the evening with his brothers; and yet none the less, our lives were imbued, shaped, directed by a sense of his will. My mother justified every choice in terms of his preference: cabbage, Yorkshire pudding, flannelette sheets, Fairy soap, an absence of magazines and such trash. His actual demands were probably not unreasonable, but mirrored in her anxious perception of his requirements they assumed gigantic proportions: to me he seemed like one of those ordinary people imaged in distorting glass in seaside booths that could evoke a fleeting terror. Ash on the hearth was his particular aversion. How often, sitting in the fender to make toast, we left a litter of crumbs, coke dust, charred crust, until hearing his key in the latch we each sprang to seize the little brass brush and tidy the hearth rather than endure his irritable remarks. No resistance was ever offered. On the contrary, there was a constant, unremitting effort to keep things smooth, so that even the baby was put to bed and tidied out of sight; or kept tied in a chair or pram or cot or play-pen.

Thus it was not possible to say no to swimming. Exercise – like fresh air – was good for the health. On Saturday afternoons we went to town on the tram with our threadbare, tightly rolled towels and our new elasticated swimming costumes. The pool was indoors, a cavernous old building, cold in the corners, full of vaporous chemicals and the echoes of voices that smacked the vaulted roof and the slippery ground and flew back in great shocks of sound that bounced around and fought each other till my head rang and I clung to my father's hand as he dragged me to the edge. I was frightened of the water, frightened of lifting my legs and lowering my chin to the lurching surface, frightened of the rough boys, frightened of their explosions of splashing, frightened of their thunderous voices, their thudding feet as they bounded along the runways, frightened of the angry man with his sharp whistle whose sudden shout – Oi you, out! – could make an instant momentary hush. But more than all these things put together I was frightened of angering my father.

I dithered too long on the edge before risking the water, and he shrugged and swam slowly away, leaving me at the mercy of these other strange dangers. Jump, he shouted. But my legs would not obey. I forced myself to double up so that I was squatting on my haunches. I encouraged one toe to touch the water. Somebody gave my shoulder a light shove and – screaming – I was in and under, my mouth ears nose eyes all full of water. I rubbed and shook my head to clear them, striving to look pleased, because my father, having given some passing stranger the nod to tip me in, was laughing. Company and action stimulated my father. He was a popular man amongst men – almost a lord of misrule. A funny man, whose clowning always contained an edge of satire, an intention. Taking me swimming came out of such an intention: exercise, like education, was a virtuous pursuit. There was nothing purely playful in this outing, no time for me to explore and find my own way. First he showed me the strokes. Then, taking hold of my head with one hand, he grasped my chin in the firm cup of his other hand and, dislodging my feet from the bottom of the bath, pulled me along, yelling at me to go through the motions with my legs and arms. This he repeated several times, and each time, just as I seemed to achieve a degree of equilibrium, he let go of my chin so that I was submerged again. In vain I pleaded with him not to let go. In vain I tried to conceal my mounting panic. Exasperated by my fear, he kept telling me that, standing, I was not out of my depth, even though whenever my feet involuntarily sought to find that out for themselves he scolded me for wasting time. After half an hour of choking and struggling with stinging eyes and throat, I was allowed to go and get dressed, while he went to swim a few lengths, before hurrying me off to the market.

My father led a crammed life. Every minute he was not working was packed with action; he never rested. The swimming bath was just next door to the market, where three or four of his brothers worked, and he wanted to go and pass the time of day. It was not in his nature to resist the chance of a chat. Perhaps my lack of zest was discouraging to him, just as his overbearing vitality was alarming to me. But whatever the reason, it seems to me that, in spite of our famous alikeness, there was always between my father and myself a failure of sympathy that gradually developed into a mutual antagonism. So when my mother asked about the swimming, there was a lack of enthusiasm on both sides that expressed itself in me as a polite stoical acceptance and in him as a grudging retort: She'll do.

Now, when I think about my father, when I think about my fear of my father, the causes tend to evaporate, and in retrospect the sense of his power appears almost mythical. And yet it was real. It was a most potent influence – for good as well as for evil. It was not a bad thing to learn swimming or, later, to be kept up to the mark in school. The trouble was that unconscious and unquestioning assumption of authority, expressed through minutiae about which, much of the time, there was a coincidence of interest between my parents, an agreement about such matters as right feeding and cleanliness, and routines for work and sleep, and the importance of good schooling, which resulted in a constant tendency to dissolve resistance in the general verdict: he is a good man after all. A good provider, my aunts would say. Clean living. Not given to drunkenness. Or women. Or foul language. His only failing – and there was a common acceptance that every man was entitled to one vice, his bit of pleasure – was gambling. But gambling within limits was venal – almost a way of saving, or certainly not losing, if you were clever enough. My father's cleverness was legendary. At work men vied to get a place on his bench because his tips were supposedly infallible. Gambling meant windfalls and treats. Gambling meant the unexpected trip and the sudden cessation of routine. Gambling broke the rigour and injected the dour working days with the flavour of adventure and independence. And winning was wonderful to my mother and me, not for the material benefits alone but because it meant a transformation in the whole atmosphere of our lives, and because the relentless concentration and preoccupation my father usually betrayed, which I now understand to be the normal state of the true addict, was transmuted into a marvellous elation.

Every evening almost there was a race meeting somewhere in the region to which he travelled in all weathers after working a ten-hour day, standing at the job, which meant the meticulous matching and cutting of expensive cloth and was thus exacting work; piece-work which paid a decent wage only if one worked fast all the time. And after this gruelling regime, which lasted fifty years, every evening he went to the dog track, studied form, placed bets, scrutinised the performances, made pencilled notes on the margins of the programmes in his spidery uncertain writing. And his mind, exercised so narrowly – with such economy of decision – was like a very very keen small instrument, which being turned to other matters was capable of piercing straight to the marrow, cutting through all the delicate tissues and integuments of feeling in order to get at the gist. If the idea was to swim, there was no point in holding back. What possible use could hesitation serve?

But she offered no opposition. And this was partly because she was in awe of his cleverness. Resistance – the least sign of argument – honed his mind to sharpness. His meanness was smallness of vision, not malice. There was no aggression in his assertion, because it never occurred to him that he might be thwarted. He believed in the moral order, the existence of right and wrong, and he was always right. His appeal to logic was irrefutable. Thus he would weigh the odds and reach his decision without apparent self-interest according to what seemed to him a natural law. Instead of engaging in conflict with this law, my mother became devious, indirect; my friend and ally, his friend and wife. Late at night I would hear them talking, he expostulating, she quietly insinuating, both voices hushed so as not to disturb my sister and myself. The imbalance between them, her subjected status, filled me with resentment, so that I could not love my father. Or, if love, it was a love adulterated by fear and anger. My mother tried to foster our friendship, his and mine. When I brought home a good report she would urge me to be the one to hand it over for him to read. But he never approved – never vouchsafed one term of praise that was gratuitous. Always he was sharp enough to detect the flaws in my performance. Always he asked: Were you top? And, quailing, I always had to admit after I went to the grammar school that I was never top. Then he seemd to turn away from me, dissatisfied, so that I never felt good enough or clever enough to please him, to escape censure and to make her feel easy in her mind. Of course, very rapidly, I knew more of certain subjects than either of my parents, but it was always clear that the raw material of my mind was, like hers, inferior, and so the extra knowledge could only cause further separation without actually enhancing my position.

Whenever he took me anywhere – like the market – where his relations or friends or work-mates might be present, I had to be particularly careful to avoid disgracing my father. My great dread was that somebody would shoot a question at me that I would be unable to answer. My mother's sisters were always saying he was proud of me because I had passed my scholarship to the grammar school. But I could sense his trepidation lest I should make a fool of myself. My status as a scholarship girl often seemed to inspire people with a desire to put me through some sort of inquisition that would end, on discovering that I could not instantly answer mental arithmetic sums, with patronising smiles. Sometimes they were joke questions – How much is a pennorth of threepenny bits? – but I would be too paralysed with fright to smile until too late. For this reason I used to pretend to be deep in thought; it was surprising how easily people were deceived by this trick. My father, on the other hand, could never be put off the scent: he had a sharp nose for a lie. Sometimes on such occasions he would demand: Have you lost your tongue? Since at other times strict silence was enjoined on me I never knew which was the best tactic and simply strove to be invisible.

But the market uncles paid no attention to me; they were my father's brothers and they shared his interests, not just his passion for gambling and sports of all kinds, but his involvement in the politics and personalities of that world. Gambling shops in those days were hole-in-corner places that were often raided by the police; such episodes would be related with great gusto. There were malpractices at race meetings to be deplored and fabulous successes to be extolled. Above all, there was an ongoing discussion of form, which meant a hair-splitting analysis of the performance of dogs and horses. The variables and permutations were infinitely fascinating to these men. Sometimes, on off-days – which meant days when business was not brisk – these conversations would not take place in the alley-way in front of the stalls, but in the den inside under the awning. There, somebody would set a sturdy orange-box for me to sit on and perhaps give me an apple. My germ-conscious mother always washed fruit, I would look desperately at my father for permission before daring to sink my teeth into the flesh and he, already in full flow, would fling at me: Yes, eat, eat. There would be a dirty tin kettle on a gas ring and big mugs of tea on a floor that was covered thickly in potato sacks for warmth. Often, two or three of the men talked together all at once, vehemently, very loudly, but not in anger. We hardly ever visited the homes of these relations, who mostly lived in council houses, and had a lot of children whose names I did not even know though they were my cousins because my mother felt out of place with his people, whereas he was completely at home with hers. As for me, once I knew I was not going to be put to the test, I was quite content to nibble at the apple and play the game: through the gap where the canvas flaps are tied with string, the oranges come first in glossy diagonals, and then the apples, the green and the streaked red, and the russet, and the little Coxes, and then the tomatoes, the soft and the hard, translucent and veined, and the pearly mushrooms. And a woman standing with a sagging bag and two ragged children dragging at her coat who asks: How much is the lettuces? Muttering, she turns away. But suddenly, like a whirlwind, my father is on his feet and shouting: Here, love, I'll pay. Shamed, the stall-keeper – my uncle is only a paid helper, not an owner – the owner will not let my father drop the shilling in the till and, chaffing each other, they split the difference, while the blushing woman protests happily and my father chunters: Nay, sixpence a piece will never break the bank.

At night I hear my parents talking in bed. The low-pitched voices rise and fall, now merging into one continuous stream, now halting. I lift my head from the pillow. If this goes on, she is urging, I shall have to get a job. What job, he is saying, what job can you do with the baby? I lie on my back, listening. What is short-time? The baby needs shoes, she is saying, and she needs a new school uniform for the new school. I'll get you some good serge, he is saying, for the gym slip. I can knit the woollens, but what about the sports equipment, my mother says, and the underwear? I pray: Please God let me not wear second-hand clothes. Yet I know it is wrong to pray for things. Please God let someone give me a racket. There are tennis courts at the park and a netball post in the old school yard, but what is hockey? The list of things I need is very long: a satchel, a pencil-case, a fountain pen of my own, name tapes made specially for me. I long for the dear little tapes with my own name embroidered in red silk. Let a rich relation suddenly knock on the door one day soon. And let this rich relation say: A dozen of everything on the dot. No, a dozen is not enough. A dozen dozen. Their voices rise and fall like waves ebbing. A dozen dozen. If only my mother was still here, she is saying. It seems so unending, this struggle.

My mother held the tape taut while I dipped the pen into the little bottle of Indian ink and wrote my name over and over again. Her youngest sister, who was a tailoress, took the strips of tape and sewed them into my new clothes with stitches so small and perfect they could have been made with a machine. If he lets me go for the interview, my mother was saying, I shall wear my best black tailor-made with the hand-stitched lapels. You do right, her sister said, if he wants his rashers of best bacon and his fillets of dover sole. He's a good provider, my mother said, when they're not working short-time, but it's not just the money. What is it then? I said. Teasing, my aunt put a finger on her nose: It's rude to chip in when your elders are talking. But if it's not just the money? It's this house, my mother said, the loneliness with your grandma gone. How will you manage, my aunt said, with the baby? In the day time, she'll go to Mrs Up-the-Road, and evenings and weekends we'll muck in together and get the housework done. Where there's a will there's a way, her sister said, that's what I always say. So now when I came back from school the house was empty. Her absence gave me greater independence and numerous duties. On work days we made no coal fire till I got home. It was my business to set the fire, tidy the house, pick up the baby from the neighbour, peel the potatoes, warm the stew in the gas ring, make the beds, but first – above all – change out of my precious uniform. My set of school clothes included one white poplin blouse which had to be dried overnight if it became soiled during the week. Often, mornings, this school blouse was airing on the fender in front of a borrowed electric fire, a one-bar heater that was switched on for only a few minutes at a time because the neighbour had warned that it was prone to overheating. In cold weather changing out of these clothes was the worst job of all. Sometimes when he came home he would give me a swift glance and then say curtly: You haven't washed your face. I suppose the coal dust had probably got on my cheeks where I might have pushed back my hair with grubby fingers. Silently and resentfully I would swill my hands under the tap. There was always a pretext for him to be critical, and because I was punctilious in observing these duties, I would hate his remarks. Sometimes with bated rage, not finding them in the proper place by the door, he would demand: Slippers! And I would realise that they had become displaced while I was sweeping and that he felt incapable of moving a step in his stockinged feet, so enslaved was he by his own rules. And the pressure of indignation at his high-handed treatment of me would make tears come to my eyes. But I would stoop down and meekly hand him the slippers and set his plate of dinner in front of him so that he could gobble up his evening meal – he was always a voracious eater – and then dash off to his meeting, moving so fast usually that since he was always served first from the pan, he was gone before we had time to seat ourselves and begin our meal.

Only much later did I begin to see that at least in part his extraordinary strength was a function of my mother's extreme docility. And part of it was simply a given – given in his ownership of the house, in the address my grandmother has known and named him by as the mester, in our assumption of his name and his protection, part of the subtle ambience of deference that pervaded all our language. That part of it was perhaps out of her control – out, even, of her consciousness, as it was for many years of mine – because so automatic and ordinary, replicated in every household in every branch of our extensive family, in every house in our street and, so fas as I knew, in all the houses in all the lands.

So, in church, the vicar, a huge broken-backed man whose black soutane was seen as a high church extravagance, and whose passionate sermons left the congregation uneasily stirred, spoke of a Father in Heaven whose absolute Love was absolute rigour, purveying a view of the Godhead that was the very double of my private vision of my own father. And if I represent him now as a poor thing, driven by circumstance, balancing out his burdens and his appetites in good faith through the long years, that charitable vision is a learned and much later addition. At the time the sentiment I cherished towards him was one of bitter repudiation; and when he entered the house, a darkness fell across our souls.

But, again, part of that power was not according to the common pattern, but was given to him exclusively and specially by my mother. Even at the time I knew this was the case, and I heard reasons, because my mother's sisters would often sit by the fire when he was absent and discuss how he had altered my mother, how he had changed her nature from that of a light-hearted girl to a jittery woman. Her youth gave him the advantage. She constantly deferred to him, with the respect of a well-brought-up child for an older person. Her own father had died in her infancy and her brothers were older and had left home before she was properly weaned; and because my grandmother still had six girls at home, they were raised in poverty that my mother found abrading and that left scars. Somehow the struggle to survive in respectability was transmuted – more in my mother's case than in any of the other children – into a desire for gentility. Perhaps the months in service were formative. The sisters would laugh that for my mother it was never enough to be fed and clean and honest, she must also be graceful, charming and singular. And though they teased her foibles, there was affection and admiration in their voices, because she was very gentle and kind and because she owned her own house and was making her way in the world. The very qualities that made her exceptional within the family gave her credence in the outside world; in time she was given responsibility at work because she had an intense respect for authority and a burning desire to be a personage.

Thus, according to her sisters, she had always wanted to marry a man with clean hands, a tradesman, not a labourer. Because my father worked with fine cloth, his hands could never touch rough tools; though they were calloused by the heavy shears he used, they were otherwise shapely and white and perfectly smooth. He wore a shirt and a suit to his work. Even before he had a bathroom of his own, he took baths at the public baths and liked to dress for best in the hand-finished clothes of his own factory where he was entitled to a discount in price. He had an umbrella and a white silk scarf with fringes, and had learned how to play chess at the Boys' Brigade, whist at church socials, fox-trots at the local dances given in aid of charity. He was gentlemanly. Being, like my mother, one of the youngest, of twelve children, he had never had a bed – or even a drawer – of his own, and he wanted to buy a house. Moreover, to an even greater extent than my mother, he had a trace of romantic recklessness in his nature. An obsessional gambler, he had let his first youth slip before he ever had time to spare for a wife, but once his attachment was formed for my mother, he first tried to shower her with presents – which my grandmother would not allow – and then, becoming engaged with a proper engagement ring, he entrusted her with all his earnings and winnings towards their future home. Together, in the months before the marriage, they must have spent all their non-working hours window-shopping. In this respect they were both idealists, idealising these possessions in a way that more sophisticated people might have called – mistakenly – materialist. For the things that they acquired were not only the outward manifestation of their own worth, as hard-working, right-thinking people, but also the proof that there was some kind of justice in the world.

Yet somehow, in spite of this important similarity, somehow there was no union. No parity. Somehow my mother remained deeply estranged. Naturally there were no quarrels, because it would not have been lady-like to indulge in squabbles. Yet in the matter of the job she had simply asserted herself and carried the day. In a sense, there was never any need for overt opposition, because in so many other matters

45

they were of like mind. On the surface all was mutual respect and consideration. Order was everywhere. In the cupboards, in the drawers, on the surfaces. Everything was done to order. The table-cloth that was too small for the table was always spread crosswise so that at each corner a neat triangle of wooden surface was exposed. Centrally the cruet and the sauce bottle, then the sugar bowl. The largest knife for him; for her the knife with the lighter bone handle, that was not so sharp, so that sometimes she had to ask him to cut her meat, choosing for herself the coarser cuts out of modesty, which he then took back on to his own plate out of chivalry, giving her and me the best bits. All this was ritualised and predictable. Except that when he went out and we sat on the fender and made crumbly, untidy toast, we licked our fingers like two children. And in a sense – she and I – we were two children, with the baby, back from the minder's evenings and weekends, dandled between us like a shared doll. And because – even though she worked and earned money and ran the house and paid the bills and planned the holidays and figured out all the arrangements and was immensely practical – because in relation to him she remained a fearful child, I caught the contagion, caught from her an exaggerated sense of his awesome power.

There were no ornaments in our house, except the fruit basket, the pair of photographs in pewter frames, a candlestick coiled like a brass cobra – no pictures, cushions, rugs, books, no casual clutter. In other houses one might see a mantelshelf with a hair-clip, two stamps, a picture postcard, three or four letters with torn envelopes, a book of matches with the flap torn and scrawled, signs that life lazed along more easily and left its droppings. In our house it was otherwise because he could not tolerate disorder. Everything must be spare, plain, bald, bare. At the beginning there was no money for inessentials since, unlike most other people, they were going to own their house. But what began as necessity was elevated to a rule, a rule she implemented and attributed to him, which he in turn upheld; and wherever there was congruence of opinion between them, things ossified, hardened, became inflexible. Between them they managed to eliminate all points of conflict, she by evasion, he by unconscious coercion. His capacity for contempt – a burning scorn – was monstrous. We could bring in a jar of buttercups to put on the kitchen window-sill and he could say with an abrupt laugh: What's that rubbish? and straight away it would be whisked into the dustbin and the stippled paint carefully wiped down with a scrap of the cotton waste workers were allowed to bring home for dusters. It was as if the constraints of the conveyor belt and the machine had the power to manufacture private strictures that could destroy even the free things in life, or as if utility was the measure of all things. Compulsion was the touchstone of our existence, of which, to us, we children – my mother and I – he seemed the guardian. And we knew that this was inevitable, because he was a working man, which meant that his own life was mortgaged to the machine.

And that is why, even now, thirty years or more since I first left home, I still ask myself: Am I doing it right? Am I doing it right? The question begins there in the hope not after all of gaining approbation, but merely of evading blame. A different kind of woman would have let the buttercups stand. A messier woman might have left the jar until the water grew stagnant and the dropped petals turned to yellow dust. There were in our district uncouth women who might have hurled the glass at his head and been beaten for their trouble. But my mother fretted and submitted. She was timid. And she wanted to be graceful. And she wanted me to be good. So I was good to please her and to keep him at bay. And to be good was to be like her – to be modest and undemanding, and when something really mattered, like her job, to be devious if necessary and to bear false witness.

My mother was kind to us both, trying to bring us together, to smooth the way for us to meet, unaware that her subordination to him created an insurmountable barrier. Once, when his hair was thinning, she brought home a special shampoo that was supposed to be massaged into the scalp. She said coaxingly: Let her do it for you. The kitchen was our one warm habitable room. He was sitting at the table in his usual place, nearest the fire, his shirt collar tucked under, his arms folded bashfully as in the photograph, his plate wiped clean with bread and pushed towards the centre of the gingham cloth to make way for the newspaper. A poor yellowish radiance streamed down from the naked bulb overhead. The marbled glass shade had broken and my mother, scrimping a replacement out of her own earnings, had hidden it in the wardrobe bottom, frightened because she had not asked his permission. Next time he had a winning stint, she would cajole him into buying a new shade, and, if he gave the money, the cheap new paper shade would come out of its hiding place. If he threatened to make the purchase himself, I would hear them at night, he teasing that he could make a better bargain, she mildly urging: But let me please because I understand colours. Colours, his voice would begin to sizzle,what am I doing all day but matching colours? And when the parchment soon became stained and discoloured in the steamy kitchen air, he would jeer: You've been diddled out of your money. Worse still, if the impulse took him in passing by the shop one day, he might even veer off course, forcing us to stand by in acute discomfiture while he berated the shopkeeper for selling inferior goods. Thus, an undercurrent of anxiety filled the kitchen with a kind of dreary tension. It was very tiring, very debilitating to be constantly submerged in these intensities of feeling. I sniffed the contents of the bottle of hair-restorer, and thin yellow oil, faintly medicated, a product of quackery, at which he of course scoffed, submitting only to humour her whim. I poured a few drops into the palm of one hand, and with my moistened fingertips tentatively touched the crown, the nape, the pink pleat behind the ears. My mother gestured in small circles, encouraging. The skin of his skull was glistening with the oil. The scalp, my mother urged. Minute scales clung to the base of each follicle. The silver-grey hair turned into leaden strands. My mother ran a bowl of cold water in the kitchen sink and added hot from the kettle. Let her shampoo it, she repeated. I hovered, embarrassed, nauseated, my hands smarmy with grease. I can do it myself quicker, he muttered, with a hasty glance at the clock. I haven't got time for this messing.

The house where my sister was minded was full of dogs and snotty-nosed children, where the chair bottoms bulged with news-papers and dishes were stacked in the sink. Her pretty dresses were taken off and replaced by dungarees, and she was allowed to play freely in the street. At home-time it was pleasant to sprawl on the floor in front of the fire at this house, to eat biscuits out of the packet and to read love-stories out of cheap magazines. My mother was never critical of other people: it was enough that the woman was kind and needy. But my sister, raised partly and partly neglected in this easier atmosphere, was not biddable like me.

My list of tasks is long and I am always late getting home from the minder's, where I love to loll on the sofa listening to the gossip. He's a proper pig, a girl giggles, he'd have me down here on the rug in the middle of us fish and chips if he could get his zip down, but he's all fingers and thumbs when he's had a skinful. At last I pick up my sister and my satchel and run down the street. First, I must peel the potatoes and drop them into boiling water or the meal will not be ready. When they are simmering I make the fire and then I fly up the stairs to change and to tidy the beds. But first I must tie my sister to a chair and give her a rusk; she struggles and protests. In a year or two it will be easier to open the back door and let her run out into the street. Now, when I finish my chores in good time, I try to cuddle her and she squirms and wriggles down off my knee on to the red rug. I long to love her, and her imperviousness is hurtful. I give her leg a very small slap. She looks startled, plumps down on her bottom and watches me for a moment. Her eyes are more knowing now. They are yellow eyes – unlike any eyes I have ever seen. Your grandmother had hazel eyes, my mother keeps saying. But my grandmother's eyes were quite different – green and flecked. I wonder what my sister is seeing with those eyes. In a moment she begins to scramble towards the fender to wave her arms at the fire. I pull her back towards me and administer another very small tap. If she begins to cry, she will let me comfort her until the hurt subsides, and then once again she will struggle to escape. But I dare not make her cry. I am afraid of hurting her, afraid of being found out. I want her to love me, but she is intent on the banging she can make with the fire irons on the fender. When the potatoes begin to bubble, and my attention is needed elsewhere, I have to tie her in the chair again, because I cannot risk her burning herself on the fire. I lift her, and she arches her spine angrily and lets out a squawk. I strap her carefully into the chair to avoid squeezing her stomach, and tickle her tears with my tongue till she begins to laugh, and then I give her a crust dipped in golden syrup.

Together, the two of us – my sister, a baby sleeping – my mother and I baking on the kitchen table, could be peaceful and harmonious and busy. On Saturday evenings we made scones, buns, tarts which would last the week. With what zest, with what a sense of anticipation my mother would sweep off the chenille cloth to reveal the white scrubbed surface. Out of the cupboards would come the canisters and tins and baking bowls, until at the height of our preparations the table would be full of clutter. My mother delighted in each part of this operation, producing pies that were decorated with rose-buds and leaves, glazed with egg and milk and frosted with granulated sugar. We basked in the warmth of the oven, the good smells of singed sugar and cinnamon and nutmeg, the crisped edges of crimped paper shells. I rubbed and whisked and scraped and licked to my heart's content. Sometimes we plumped raisins in hot water to make them fat and juicy, and sometimes we pressed coconut mixtures into egg-cups to make macaroons which would insist on collapsing on the tray. My mother was entirely taken up by these operations, tirelessly, zealously intent on creating good things which would all be demolished within a few days.

But before he returned everything must be returned to order, for whenever he was present there was always that dangerous friction. And above all, as I grew older, I began to resent his failure to be the friend she wanted him to be. There was a loneliness in my mother, a generous susceptibility that never met its match. In all her leisure hours, while he was with his brothers and mates, she was alone – except for her children. Even her sisters could not call in the evenings, for they in turn had to stay in their houses with their children. In the long empty summer evenings she kept herself busy in the house and in the yard; and in the winter we stayed in the kitchen near the fire. Sometimes when he was absent, when we sat in the half-dark listening to the radio, she knitting by touch, me crouched on the hearth trying to read by the dim fire-glow, it was very like those afternoons by the seaside with my grandmother – warm, peaceful, absorbing, timeless; different only because, being older, I surfaced now and then, coming back into the here and now. Then I found myself when she, looking at the luminous numerals on the clock face, began to wonder whether he had missed the last train or tram, startled by a fierce, forbidden hope that used to spring up like a sudden conflagration, and I used to pray, silently, fervently: Let him never come home.

Four

Weeks pass. Weeks and weeks while I write these pages. Most of the time is consumed not by writing, but by domestic activities, in the lulls of which I find myself sitting in the one comfortable kitchen chair, the chair I usually read in while I am waiting for something to cook; only just at present I am not reading – not during these weeks. Two preoccupations keep me absorbed in calculations, two concerns that are in constant conflict: whether to go on living in this way and to gain what fulfilment I can out of my own creativity, or whether to take active steps to alter the externals of my existence. These alternatives constantly throw up fresh configurations, depending partly upon immediate stimuli, partly upon ongoing processes of thought – patterns which are deeply absorbing, fantasies of escape, and adventure, of fabulous success, of profound peace, of tremendous discovery, fantasies which connect me with the girl brooding darkly all those years ago, longing for a freedom which at best I could conceive only in negative terms: the absence of my father. Extraordinary flights of rhetoric accompany these dreams; or elaborate debates in which both sides indulge in eloquent arguments on their own behalf, leaving me exhausted without being satisfied. At night, when I finally go to bed, I promise myself the question will settle itself and that on the next day I shall set in motion a course of events that must inevitably follow from that decision. But I fall asleep as soon as my head touches the pillow, and the next day I spend myself on the diurnal round until again comes a lull and again I fall into the internal mesh and sit there, in my chair, enthralled, intent, deeply and privately involved in this dialogue of the divided will.

And when at last, putting aside argument, I come back to these pages, everything that has already been set down seems still-born, disfigured. I detect imperfections not in the style merely, but in the actual sense of the writing: false emphases, distortions of the past, infringements of the truth. I flinch at this opening up of the whole question of objective reality, but cannot disguise from myself my – possibly old-fashioned – belief that events did have a certain verity; and that it is my duty to be true to these facts. It is as if I still believe that the items that were once transferred from the seashore to my frock pockets and from my pockets into my mind continue to exist, but only so long as I keep bringing them to life. To perform that miracle I need only tell the truth. Thus, it is as if the truth has some talismanic virtue; as if by being faithful to the word I can not only resurrect these buried lives, but also achieve my own salvation.

Increasingly, the outside world became identified with his domain. And as with him, so in all my dealings with that world in those early years, fear was the dominant note. The scholarship that took me into the wider world was important to my father and mother. To me it meant a uniform, a bus-ride, an intimidatingly large building, a lot of new people, and the knowledge that I had gratified my parents' expectations, for whom the scholarship represented a passport to a better life. Having no general conception of life, I merely enjoyed the temporary aura of success that his satisfaction produced. For my mother, the scholarship was simply to appease my father. Her love was not contingent upon success. But that my success was crucial was never in doubt. She often told me he was proud of me. But with the knowledge of his satisfaction came the renewed fear of losing it, so that learning, during all those years of early girlhood until I was some sixteen years old, took place in an atmosphere of oppression. Going into the long high corridors of that school was like losing my grandmother out of bed on a dark night, was like standing in the attic holding my dear dead cousin's embroidery, was like letting go my mother's hand on a steep slope, or confronting alone my father's obdurate intelligence, a form of terror that could be survived only by being very still and small and insignificant. It was as if within those high, blank, brick walls, so peculiarly devoid of plaster, paper, paint, so blatantly structural and cold, I was entrapped as in a prison; and though I was supposed to be a clever girl, I felt stupefied by this experience – dulled, blunted, and nullified.

I had no conception of an alternative universe. There was no other life. I had no will of my own. I was not even aware of lacking volition.

Everything was organised – school and home – and that left no spaces in which the will could operate, except between one destination and another, or alone in bed, or in those leisure hours when I was allowed to read a book, although reading itself was a permitted exercise of the will, since one would hardly choose to sit in vacancy. It was not that there was no pleasure in reading or in the domestic and scholarly activities; it was simply that everything that happened happened without my permission. Imagine a puppet with the faculty of reasoning, its little jointed arms and legs twitched ceaselessly by strings, worked on by a tireless operator, its puppet-thoughts constantly intercepted, its vague puppet yearnings never allowed to take proper shape, always jiggled and jolted into action by an ignorant animator. Such was my condition. I never remember speaking or acting of my own accord. And I remember that the relative seclusion and peace of the private world of home was a refuge at this time from the incomprehensible demands of that outer life, which seemed to present ever-widening circles of unimaginable terror. And it is this deep deep sense of incompetence that – it seems now – divides my mind against itself, leading me to this very point, where even now I am still unable to make a choice.

Weeks pass. I sit in the kitchen, watching the clock for a cake, consumed by these tasks, but always, beneath, there is this continuum, this obsession to shape, to recover, to reshape, to make a meaning. The game goes on; and thus I experience my life as a whole in spite of its divisions and gaps, its dreadful losses. And I feel a perilous urgency, as if I am the guardian of precious substances that I am protecting from utter annihilation. The part of me that was shaped by those domestic routines feels supported, deeply reassured to be in the kitchen, within the home. I pile laundry into the washing machine, close the door, set the timer, listen to the throb of motor as the rotors turn and tumble, and I feel rooted, secure. At the same time my mind springs to attention. Everything is grist to the mill. Nothing must be lost. If I rest, if I sleep, if I die, if the I of the me ceases to be, the world will be annihilated. There is – I sometimes fear – something absurd in this heroic conception, but my self-consciousness, my trick of mocking this effort, is itself one of the wounds I carry with me from the past. It is my father in myself, asking: What is the point? Will it put butter on your bread? Will it put roses in your cheeks? Will it do you good?

The scholarship entitled me to choose from two schools: one was in the city centre, the other, which my parents chose because it would provide plenty of good fresh air, stood on the outskirts in its own extensive grounds. Of the sixty or so children at my primary school only six were lucky enough to gain a place, and of these six the others all elected for the school near home. In the first week, my greatest fear was of getting lost, and my next was of letting anybody see my mother take me to the bus, but by and by she asked an older girl from our neighbourhood to let me tag along with her, until she was sure I knew the way.

The summer before I started at the new school was the last time I ever played with the children of the street, though those of us that came from the most respectable homes had never played in the alley-way itself, but in each other's yards. In the war the street had seemed timeless. I had gone away each summer but the street stayed the same: some fifty houses, brow to brow, tall so that except at the very height of day one side of the canyon was always in deep shadow. The top half of the street, where I lived, had been constructed between the wars; the bottom half was built in the nineteenth century like all the other streets. Most of these older houses belonged to landlords, but the new houses and a few of the others were owner-occupied, like ours. These first residents had known a brief period of relative prosperity before the war: the Jews were skilled operators, like my father; some of the others were small shopkeepers. There was a taxi-driver and a plumber and a bus-inspector and even an old lady who was reputed to have been an infant headmistress and who wore beautiful felt hats that came from a smart millinery. The chemist lived above his premises. A pair of maiden sisters kept the shop at the top corner. There was a single man who had once been a chimney sweep and who, having been wounded in the first war and getting a pension, had somehow managed to wangle himself into the possession of six back-to-back houses in another street. He was a notoriously bad landlord – but there was no such thing as a good landlord. According to my aunts, they were always trying to raise the rents or to evade mending the property or to get people out in order to get other people in, so that to own a house was a great blessing. In the streets therefore I had belonged to a privileged minority, but the scholarship tipped the balance against me: overnight I became a snob in the eyes of these neighbourhood children – and, indeed, for a long long time, in mine.

But the street was not the same. After the war the privately owned dwellings had begun to change hands. Many of our neighbours had been Jews and they were on the move. The people next door went to America. Another family went to South Africa. Others migrated outwards towards my new school, and this became the object of my mother's aspiration. People were beginning to say that the district was going downhill because some of the original tenants were rehoused in new council estates and foreign families moved into their places: Poles and Latvians and Lithuanians. Sometimes the tenanted houses emptied mysteriously overnight, the rent not paid, the backyards full of trash. Once, waking very early in the morning when it was just beginning to be dawn in the sky, I heard the clop of hooves. I listened for the clink of the milk bottles, but there was no other sound – except the wind banging a door. Finding that I wanted to go, I crept into the bathroom. It was too cold to sit on the seat, because the window was open to let out the germs, and as I hovered I heard the horse again, a snuffling sneeze this time, then a stagger, followed by a sharp whoa. The hinges on the bathroom window were stiff. Very cautiously and gently I pushed, and then I leaned out to look. The people opposite were bringing out their belongings to pile on a small flat cart, a two-wheeler. The horse was in the shafts and the boy of the house was holding a blanket or a cloth of some sort over its head to keep it quiet.

Sometimes, when a house was almost beyond redemption, the council came and took possession, and after a rough job of renovation a slum clearance family would be moved in temporarily until a proper corporation house could be found. And sometimes such a family would be unregenerate and would quickly reduce their temporary dwelling to a slum. So, in this house directly opposite ours, where soldiers had encamped during the war, a man and his wife and son had been placed whose presence became a plague to my mother. My mother was terrified of violence, and the couple were constantly fighting; the boy never went to school and the ever-open door gave on to a kitchen of indescribable squalor. In my infant days I had tottered up the back steps of almost every house and in through every back door, seldom to venture beyond the door-mat, to be given pennies and biscuits, to be taken on the knee of the lady of the house and have ribbons tied, to trot after the mester into the yard and steal a peep at the shy brown rabbits that were being fattened for stew, to run errands for my grandma to the corner shop and to be let inside grudgingly after hours, to be given dry eggless cakes flavoured with caraway seed at the next-door neighbour's house at Passover, to tiptoe into the head-teacher's posh sitting room and touch the silky white keys of her black piano and to let her hear me read and to hear her say in a tiny strangled voice: Very good, now, run along dear. The family that was flitting did not belong in such a street. Secretly, they carried out their traps. It meant they were lawless people fleeing in the night from debt to some further destitution. For my mother's sake I was glad they were going, but it was pitiful to see them struggling to balance their wretched bedding on a cart with no sides.

A few days after I arrived at the new school we were led into a science laboratory and told to seat ourselves in alphabetical order. The girl next to me asked me my name, but though I replied I did not think of asking for hers in return, which she however volunteered. Sylvia Martin. She had blue eyes, a wide freckled face with a low peaked brow and very pink cheeks. Her fingers were interlaced on the bench, small hands with tapering fingers, shiny skin faintly mottled with mauve. Perhaps it was cold in the laboratory, which was full of curiously shaped objects that the teacher called apparatus. We sat through the lesson and then filed out in awed silence on to a corridor where the staircase had iron railings. As the girls pooled there, while the trickle slowly descended, obeying the rule of single file, she said: Have you got a friend? And when I replied negatively she said: Will you be my friend? Clearly I knew the meaning of this word in a dictionary sense, but I had never received such a proposition. The children of the street. Were those playmates friends, or did friendship entail other benefits and conditions? I had never had any affiliation except with cousins, and cousins could not be called friends. Otherwise I had always been solitary. The girl's request seemed bold to me. My heart began to beat very fast. I wanted to think before I answered. To my horror I mumbled: I shall have to ask Doreen Black. When? she persisted. At playtime. And somebody nearby jeered: She called it playtime. Not playtime here, you big baby, break.

Immediately I was angry with myself for invoking the name of the girl with whom I travelled to school on the bus. Immediately I realised that hiding behind this excuse was babyish. The staircase led down into the white-washed basement where the free milk stood on slatted benches, each batch of bottles labelled with a class number. A monitress made us stand still to drink and then we were allowed to stroll out of doors in grounds that seemed big as a park. I finished and began to edge away but Sylvia Martin dogged my steps. I had to find the girl I had named. She was a big Jewish girl in a higher class and she had her own cronies; they were an exclusive group. When I muttered: She says will I be her friend, the big girl's brown eyes widened with what looked like disbelief. Then she shrugged crossly: I don't care what you do. Until that moment I had stayed near her because she was the only familiar face, and I was frightened of getting lost. I was not sure whether living in the next street constituted a bond or whether I had only used her name as a delaying tactic. I was very surprised to be chosen by Sylvia Martin, and, when I thought about it, relieved, because I did not know what to do with myself – other than read – in the breaks. By the end of that day Sylvia Martin was established as my friend, and during all the years that she remained at the school she was my chief recourse against the terrors of that world. Yet always, as at the beginning, it was she that supplied the impetus and the ideas, while I continued passive, receptive and – inevitably – dependent.

Within a week we had made ourselves a den in a beech hedge. At one time marking the boundary between a shrubbery and a field – the latter had eventually become school playing fields – the hedge was old, tall and thick with a stout fence inside it was made of posts and horizontal bars. It had been planted in the correct manner, with a double row of saplings at regular staggered intervals, and so it was possible literally to force a way inside the hedge, which, being several feet in thickness, felt like a fortress. We found our point of access at a break in the foliage on the shrubbery side, which meant worming our way in under bushes of rhododendron. Inside, a length of fencing remained intact, providing us with a seat on which we could sit with our feet off the ground and our knees touching our chins. It was necessary to make a dash under the bushes to reach this haven because the shrubbery was actually out of bounds. This rule enforced quietness and stillness upon us once we were safely ensconced, and we had to whisper and listen for every footfall. Such an infringement of rules would have been inconceivable for me, but my friend constantly thought of doing things – like drawing in her rough book – things which always proved to be worth the risk. And though I cannot remember a single word of those whispered conversations, I can recall with utter completeness the scratch of twigs, the unfurling of new leaves from their coppery sheaths, the fine feathered edges, the shrill of a whistle on the invisible field, the measured tread of teachers' footsteps along the driveway to the swimming pool, the shouting of voices in the school yard, the feel of my not-often-washed knees under my chin, dusty and scaly and cold.

It was at that time that I discovered living things, a whole new dimension that had nothing to do with the social world, but which I chanced upon because sometimes, to save my bus-fare, I walked to school, and that meant I could buy an iced bun with my tuppence. I was always ravenous. The houses along the route had gardens. For years we had gone for walks and my mother had pointed out the best gardens, had said with such reverence: How wonderful to see a weeping willow. Suddenly, the first spring in the new school, the trees were in bloom and I picked up broken bits of blossom and I looked and saw inside their miniature cups a structure of living tissues, diverse, intricate, harmonious, miraculously brilliant. From that time things changed. I began to see that I was seeing, to know that I was being, and to be able to revoke these random impressions. I began to play the game in earnest – not involuntarily and incidentally, but with a passionate commitment, seeking out opportunities to be alone so that I could continue where I left off thinking. Yes, at last I gave it a name, this game. I called it thinking. It was as if quite suddenly I became more conscious. At times the world seemed full of a mysterious effulgence. And it was as if this illumination, this rapture, was ultimately the real reality, a possibility for being that was constantly interrupted by false systems and contrary prescriptions. I stood in the street, holding a handful of petals, palest pink like the baby shawl, faintly patterned with veins, like the skin of the baby that was all covered in down, down, down, while a light wind shook the boughs above my head and other petals drifted, turning and turning as they fell, down, down, down, but not that down, another down, down, and all the while telling myself hurry, hurry; and, terrified of ever being naughty, I never was late, but always managed to slip into my seat in time.

Then the world seemed a miracle. Every breath brought in its wake a stream of sensations. Glory. Glory. To sit in lessons in the lulls between spells of work when the class was still intent and the teacher herself seemed to sit dreaming, in a classroom high on the second floor, a corner room with windows facing two ways, full of light, and a vast vista across parkland, wooded slopes, a valley filled with the geometric patterns of wet slate roofs, while under my very nose rain pelted on millions of leaves, was to be transported into a zone of deep, pleasurable contemplation. And though this ecstasy was solitary and could in no way have been communicated to a single living soul, it was akin in some way to the communing in the hedge with that other girl, akin because it depended for its pleasurable quality upon a state of non-coercion.

Sometimes it seems to me that if I fail those children in the hedge, that old woman lying in the creamy crimped silk of that blond oak box in that narrow street, my life will all have been so much waste and ash. Why is it not enough that it happened? Why must I make my mark? Do I still lack conviction that I ask these questions? Somehow those early years became the precondition of a consciousness split so disastrously that as the child became a girl child and then a girl, the passivity that was encouraged as the norm began to manifest itself to me as an increasing paralysis of the will. I began to know that I was only cooperating. I began to find this process increasingly tiresome. I began to be afraid of my own decerebration. There was nothing I wanted to do – except conform to their expectations. As for these mystical moments, they were bubbles – luminous, but evanescent, moments of vision that could not transform a whole existence.

Suddenly I recall that in those conversations in the hedge we had only one subject: Love. Love was the great shaping idea in all our discourse. Love was the magnet that drew our thoughts. For each of us – for me, for her, for most girls in our class – there was always a he. We lived in different sectors of the city and never met at home. Each he, therefore, remained a stranger to the other girl. And in reality, these unwitting objects of our fantasy were largely fictitious, creations of our imagination and our need. Of course, each one was a real person, but there was very little correlation between these actual figures and our figments. As individuals they no longer have the least significance, but as representatives of our rooted expectation of one day, very soon, acquiring real lovers, they were profoundly important. Because already then, at little more than childhood, the unit of our thinking was the couple.

What energy, what inventiveness, what wanton speculation went into the creation of our imaginary partners. At night I slept alone in the bed I had shared with my grandmother. The big double bolster balanced upon my body became his body. Inert, unheavy, it produced only a puzzling void. But while, physically, our idea of the couple remained cloudy, there was no confusion about the meaning of that coupling, for he was to be the perfect counterpart, rapt participant, sharing breath by breath the deeps and peaks of intimate union. This was to be the ultimate sharing, an exquisite abandonment of identity, mystical, sanctified. And there was ample authority for this assumption: for was not the Church the bride of Christ? If marriage was a fit symbol of this sacred mystery, it must itself incorporate a solemn beauty that, somehow, the wedding garments, white, veiled, cloudy with fern and strange, seamless lilies, seemed only to confirm. For weeks we cut out pictures of brides, dressed paper dollies, draped ourselves privately in old net curtains. In church I substituted his name for that of God in all the hymns and prayers and psalms and songs of praise – glory, glory – and all the fervour, incense and candle flames and embroidered altar cloths and deep reverberant music, all the solemn, other-worldly things, became emblems of that passion.

At the same time, everyday things became increasingly difficult, irksome, onerous. Lessons claimed only the surface of my mind. Only my fear of my father kept me working – to complete homework and revise for examinations. Between specific tasks there was no involvement and no commitment. Nothing made intellectual sense. The different disciplines were frameworks imposed upon a reality that was vast, multifarious, diverse and yet entire, but these rigid demarcations turned everything into inert material. To learn these subjects seemed foreign, bizarre, unneedful, subjects which – for most of my family – were at best mere names. Physics, Latin, Botany – I could see my aunts' faces registering a polite incomprehension; and often one of them would say quite fretfully: But it's not necessary for a girl. My youngest aunt would make jokes at my expense, twitting me for my long words: We used to have one, she would titter wittily, but the wheel came off. But my mother would look scared at this irreverence, warning me that my father would expect a good report. And never doubting this fact, I plugged on doggedly, but dully, content if I could achieve a middling mark and so hold on to my place in the top class, where there was no actual intellectual curiosity but only a thin, smart competitiveness for position between the cleverest girls, which left most children out in the cold. I never felt I understood enough of their language to know how to compete for the honour of first place. Dutifully I tried to please, but it was always a struggle. My inner life was like a drug. I kept weakening, letting myself go, drifting into my own amorphous thoughts. At night it was a relief to get to bed, to escape into the white drowsy tent of dreams. At dinner-time it was the den. There was no making this den, which was simply a hollow space in the hedge. The making was all in the talking. By the summer, when the grounds no longer seemed so big and strange, the den itself was no longer needed. Our compact, our togetherness, was the den. In the long lunch-time break it was possible to sit in the open field, to lie on the grass, talking. And sometimes simply staring straight up into the empty sky, thinking: There is no end to space; no end, no end.

Even now, after all these long years of living with myself, it is difficult to write about my own body. To talk, yes, because talking is fluid – the words wash away, leaving no tell-tale traces. But to write is another matter. In a sense I had no body. I never used the word. Even in the formulation 'somebody' I always substituted 'someone'. At some point in infancy it must have been instilled into me that the body was taboo, but of this process I have no recollection. I only knew that I had always been clumsy and timid. To my father's disgust, I was poor at games, never chosen for teams, always sluggish and reluctant to be engaged. Running alarmed me and ball games were an invariable humiliation. Eating was no great pleasure, though I was always hungry. Much of the food at school was of poor quality – coarse, ill-seasoned, badly cooked and cold – and we were forced to clear our plates, so that meal-times were associated with queasiness and a turbulent sociableness that curtailed the peaceful times in the den. At home, though the food was good and plentiful, the occasions were tense and emotional, and the natural functions associated with digestion – belching, farting, excreting – all unmentionable. Bathing once a week in two inches of tepid water took all the pleasure out of being clean; and mostly – especially in winter when it was cold upstairs – I remained unwashed except for my face and hands. Before being allowed in the gymnasium or swimming pool our feet were inspected. Furtively, in the privacy of cubicle or lavatory, I used to suck my shirt laps till they were soaked, and would frantically scrub between my toes and at my grubby knees and elbows for fear of being ordered loudly to the cloakroom to wash.

As for sex, there was not even a word to describe this region, which was simply unthinkable, so that though as a small child I had been regularly tubbed with cousins of both sexes, rubbed and dubbed by my grandmother with no ceremony, had discovered with fidgety fingers the small pleasurable zone just at the point of cleavage, and though I had been informed about the process of reproduction, the subject remained ambiguous. I did not really understand that the neat pleat between the legs was really the beginning of a passage that led deep into the body. In retrospect I can suppose that much of the restlessness, the irksomeness of being cooped within the confines of a desk and chair, the sense of being physically encased, restricted, might have been sexual in origin; and though at the time I made no such connection, I see now that many of us sat with our chests pressed against the wooden desk edge, or our hands clasped in our laps in jaded concentration, driven constantly against the grain. But these matters were all taboo. Earlier, when there were boys as well as girls in the classes, there had been jokes, sometimes crude language, words scrawled with chalk on the asphalt, things shouted and whispered, sometimes punishments for these crimes, as when a row of boys was lined up to be caned on the hands for looking down a girl's dress. But amongst the girls I now consorted with at school and church, there was no discourse of sexuality. Our romantic fantasies were entirely etherialised. Our biology lessons dealt with rabbits. Nothing connected with nothing. My big white bolster was a dismembered symbol of cerebral passion, a human blank, a mirror image of my own bodiless desire.

Now I recall that when I was learning to read in school, I discovered the word skill in a fairy story. Reading must have come in a flood. There is a classroom with a black stove. A fire-guard round the stove. And on the brass rail wet knickers – rinsed out in the cloakroom and wrung out to dry by the fire. The new girl who has wet her knickers has to sit on a buffet in the corner. The teacher is wearing a blue smock covered in cornflowers. She has a thick black pen and she is forming letters on a big white page that is pinned to the wall for everybody to see: The cat sat on the mat. She makes her words with a stiff, wide mouth. The children chant: The cat sat on the mat. But my grandma has already taught me my letters and I am reading a fairy story out of a thin book with stiff pages and short lines. Each page has a black and white drawing but there are also some coloured pictures. My delight in these illustrations is so great that I am in a state of rapt excitement as I turn the page, which fuses with a feeling of suspense about the outcome of the story. The prince has long yellow hair like a girl and a tiny cap with a feather. He wishes to marry the princess. But first, says her father the king, you must show me your skill. What is skill? I want to ask the teacher about this new word. Whenever you want to know something you must put up your hand and wait till you are asked, says my grandma. But there is a problem. Suppose skill is a rude word? Suppose skill is the book-word for the thing the prince needs to marry the princess? I am aware that for two people to marry there must be this rude unmentionable thing. But unless I ask, I cannot get past this line. A feeling of hot shame fills me. The teacher might be cross and scold me, for she has already shouted aloud about the wet knickers. Full of trepidation I put up my hand, but I am unable to say the word. Panic makes me want to go. I point to the mysterious word but the teacher misunderstands. You want to go, she says hurriedly, then go before you have an accident. I go. It is a relief to sit on the little low white pot in the tiny cubicle. I do not like to lock the door which swings invitingly open. I look longingly at my coat hanging on the peg. But I am not allowed to go home. I lift up my knitted pixie bonnet so that I can take a quick peep at the picture of a marigold on the wall. A page or two later I understand that skill is shooting arrows or killing a dragon with a sword. I feel very relieved that I have not asked the shameful question and at the same time I guess that it was naughty of me even to make such a mistake. Nobody must ever know that such thoughts infest my mind, especially since I am actually a good girl. The fear that the teacher might prove to be an unkind person – in spite of the blue cornflowers and the silky cross-stitches across the yoke of her smock – mingles with the dregs of sour milk in the dwarf milk-bottles in the crate near the fire-place, so that even when I have worked out the right answer I continue to feel slightly sick and ashamed.

On the big open field it was pleasant to lie and speculate – especially about love and beauty; or alone in my room – awake in the twilight – to dream of mysterious encounters. But sometimes my head emptied itself of all these things and began automatically to play the game. A blank mind – a clean, empty space – and then, beginning from the edges of my own body, I could construct the whole universe. First the white hills of the pillow, warp and weft, translucent with washing, then the tendril of a lazy daisy stitch, pallid leaves, the sheet on a summer evening billowing with restless heaves, a moth-like feather lifting with a breath of air, a sigh, a silence, a listening house where the invisible dead prevail but do not reveal their mystery. At night it never went beyond the walls of my bedroom, because between my own self and those walls there was so much to record, so much surface, so much detail, such a riot of implications, that I was constantly missing a tuft here, a tussock there, threads and starts that led in a thousand directions so that it was impossible ever to know where to begin, how to arrange an order of precedence. It was like filling a brimming cup. I was always turning back to find a bigger and better receptacle, and then again to begin again, engrossed, obsessed, even now and then closing my eyes and then opening them again to surprise the room into disclosing its secret pattern. And as each evening dwindled and dusk gave place to darkness it was necessary to keep on searching, even – especially – in the void, because the game itself was like a talisman that could keep at bay the power of darkness, the hideous knowledge that beyond those dissolving walls stretching away and away for ever was a vast expanse of night.

These memories are specks preserved in consciousness like those tiny insects trapped in amber that recall lost aeons. The fullness of things made time seem endless. Suddenly I seemed to have been in love for ever and the burden of waiting had become intolerable. It was a romantic passion, attached almost arbitrarily to a server at church – pale, slender, dark-eyed, who, in his robes, the black cassock with the white surplice, at the altar, in the light of candles, resembled an angel out of one of the coloured plates in the testament. He, the object of this passion that had been in the process of making ever since the moment when the perfume of a small, violet-coloured tablet still clung to my smeared licked palm – and perhaps even before memory – became the subject of our long communings in the den. He, who had almost no actuality beyond that of an apparition, became central in our conversations. He was a figment in human dress. And as my counterpart, he was immensely important. Without his existence, life would have seemed a series of disconnected episodes. To wake to no such presence was to experience the void. By day, it was always there, that blue, transparent infinitude. Sleeping, it lay all around, beyond the narrow bed, that night beyond night. But he filled that vacancy. He rescued me from the magnitude of time and space. He gave, all unwittingly, a form, a meaning, a direction to my life. He was the prime mover, god-like. I was under his sanction. Actually, he was scarcely aware of my existence, except as a girl of his age at the church, which he attended. But there was another, higher, more mysterious dimension, in which he completed my being. In meditating constantly upon the fulfilment of this spiritual rapport it was possible to achieve an ecstasy that was transcendent, so that constantly I moved about like a sleep-walker, in a kind of dream, poised always on the verge of revelation.

Kneeling in church, his face before my eyes, his white skin tinged with gold in the candlelight, his fist smudged with shadow, clenched nervously around the brass candlestick, the big brass cross held high on its gleaming pole, his black boots protruding shinily from under the black robe, I felt myself swooning with rapture. Everything was swept into this radiance: the polished tessellated floor of the central aisle, the rows of ashen chairs, each with hymn and prayer book ranged in order, the wooden rafters that resembled a great floating ark, the lime-washed walls, the pointed windows with muted green panes. Every-thing existed in a condition of perfect clarity. I wanted to lie on the floor. To stroke the tiles. To slither along on my belly, rubbing my heat against the smooth, cool floor. My breasts burned. Under the blue cobwebs of my knitted jumper, white silk shapes breathed and burned. My eyes clung to his cheeks, nestling in the hollows under the cheekbones. After the service I fled wildly through the streets, the segs on my heels ringing on the cobblestones, my face stinging with the cold, panting, my heart racing, wanting to shout, to beat my feet on the flags, to bang my head against the wall as if to crack myself open and spill out into the universe, anything, anything to reach some fusion, some consummation. Then, at the top of my own street, pausing, knowing that in a moment at my own yard I should need composure to protect me against exposure, knowing without being told that this violent feeling would be censured, questioned, ridiculed, excoriated; pausing with the wind tugging my coat edges, flinging a few drops of frosty rain, which spattered on the glass of the street lamp; pausing and seeing the drops on the glass, starring the glass which was full of golden light from a small gas flame, a lamp like a golden rose on a short strong stalk. Had I ever truly seen a rose except in picture books and greetings cards? Pausing, the street lined with its privet hedges, the washing lines hung with droplets of moisture, like strands of beads threaded irregularly, looped across the yards, the leaves blackened with soot which even then puffed out trails of smoke from fire-backs heaped with coal. The lives. The lives. I walked slowly, soberly, imprinting it all, every detail, every moment. The threadbare curtains staining the squares of light – buff, beige, blue, cream, green, rose – luminous panels, behind which I could envisage them all at their business, at their bickerings, at their fretful rituals: kettles simmering on hobs, cocoa powder in plum-coloured tins, tea in caddies, biscuit barrels, night ceremonies, hair in curlers, clothes airing in warm kitchens, discarded newspapers folded under bulging seats, rag rugs, dog hairs on bursting cushions. No end. No end. My heart was stretching to infinitude. Inside there was nothing. A space. A void. A dreadful absence. I reached my gate. The creak of the hinges would tell them I was coming. No time. No time. Slowly I dragged my feet along the concrete path which my grandmother had partly broken up with a hammer to make a garden border where she planted pansies, night-scented stock, michaelmas daisies and one red-hot poker. No time to summon her spirit. No time to revoke my dead cousin. The door. Across the street the lamp spattered with stars of rain. I thought: It is all spinning away from us all the time, the night, the street, the wet, the light. The people. I thought: I shall never let it go. I vowed: Let me die if I ever betray this moment.

Yes. I have kept faith. I do remember. And as these weeks pass, as I sit by the cooking pots playing the waiting game, watching the clock, checking as the potatoes come to the boil and the minute hand gives another click, click, click, I feel these minutes are like the links in a chain that binds me to a past that is constantly being eroded by time, like a monster eating its own substance. My grandmother was gone, my cousin was gone, the castles by the water: all gone. Even last year's leaves that lay on the ground like spilt blood: all gone. But the game – the labelling game – was the beginning of salvage. Those periods of conservation and reflection between the moments of ecstasy, the mere process of defining, could bestow a kind of calm, a conviction that all was not lost. Night after night, this act of preservation, defining, refining. There was an intellectual pleasure in this activity that was different from reading, more taxing, more dangerous. Because sustaining the equilibrium while remaining conscious demanded an effort of will and concentration whereas in books it was possible to achieve oblivion. Freedom from the self. The blankness of self. And thus it was a time of great mental adventures when no other excursions into experience were permitted. Earning a living, going out into the world, all that was still a long way off. Externally, everything was dictated. By day there was the regimen of school. In the evenings I came home to a list of tasks: make the fire, peel the vegetables, put a low light under the stew, brush the hearth, make the beds, dust the ledges, sweep the kitchen floor, shake out the rug, then set the table. But first, year in year out, I had to collect my sister from a neighbour's house, and sometimes I could not tear myself away from the talk, and then I let my sister play in the street so that I could frantically complete all the tasks or read while the potatoes simmered and the new fire rustled. And sometimes, too hungry to wait for the meal, I devoured whatever I could find: crackers, butterfly buns, slices of bread with scrapings of margarine and lemon curd. And sometimes I made brittle toffee out of fat and sugar and vinegar that Ginny had taught me how to make, toffee like cloudy brown glass with a coating of yellow grease. And then I thought about my cousin and shed a few tears and gorged the toffee until all the guilty evidence of greed was gone. And because I was often ravenous, restless, excited – as if I was encaged in a place that was too small and was being pushed outwards, beating against invisible barriers – while I gobbled biscuits I had a book to my nose and was devouring words, possessed by curiosity, caught and held by realms that appeared stunningly real, which turned the kitchen into a vague limbo.

There, in the end, I remained for a long while, alone in this familiar world of home and school. Home. School. Home. School. Walking home with an uncertain report, it would seem to me that if the appraisal in the sealed brown envelope were to be very bad, if his anger were to be turned upon me, the anger that was never vented, never experienced except in the affectionate, anxious gaze of my mother's soft eyes, I should have no alternative but to kill myself. I imagined first my own annihilation (a stone angel in a graveyard), then their pity and sorrow. I envisaged a state in which, reunited with my grandmother, my dead cousin and all my dead relations, I should be troubled no longer. I saw myself, dead, decomposing. I smelled the wet earth, and the wet stones, the yellow lumps of clay under the coarse tattered grass. I wondered whether my grandmother would already have become a bundle of bones. I tortured myself with the thought of her worm-infested carcass. I walked along the streets, muttering, cursing, weeping, believing that if only we could get free of him, the dreadful need to achieve excellence would be expunged. Driven. Driven. Driven to justify. Aware of him as a rod and a scourge. Aware of him as a heroic figure whose capacity, limited and frustrated by poverty, by ignorance, by responsibility, had been handed on to me as my birthright, as a sacred trust, my grandmother repeating so many times in those far-off days: She's her father's girl. So that I owed it to him as a daughter to a good father to meet his need by securing for myself a safe place in the world outside, and inside within the pale of his approval.

Once or twice, when I forgot my latch key, I had to run to the factory after school. It was like a descent into hell. In this region of densely populated streets and mills, the largest factory of all was the one where both of my parents and many of my relations worked, a huge tract of ground laid out with interconnecting sheds as big as our city station, and similar in construction, with glass roofs, naked walls criss-crossed with pipes and girders, and full of all manner of machinery and conveyor belts that made a deafening commotion. In a glass booth at the entrance to the main mill-yard sat a man in uniform, who gave permission to enter, whereupon it was necessary to penetrate the wide, greasy yard, past the furnaces where Ginny's father had been a rat-catcher and stoker, past many entrances, out of which at the siren's sound debouched great surges of men and women, fighting with each other to be foremost, past the basement windows, where no daylight ever entered and where my mother worked as a clerk. Scared of slipping on concrete worn smooth by thousands of feet and oiled by the polluted moisture that filled the air, I could see inside doorways the ravel of machinery, the pink blur of hundreds of faces, and the little glass boxes where the commissionaires kept watch over the comings and goings and over the workings of the clocking-out machines. Then my father was fetched out to me, for I was not allowed to enter. Shyly, he brought me the key. In that huge place, a small man after all, white, worn, agitated, vexed. It was a paradox that he, the dragon guarding my life, should be a prisoner in that industrial wilderness. And the realisation that this was so was the final undoing of my childhood, for I felt – standing there, bidden by the man in uniform, chidden by my father for my forgetfulness, weak, cold, hungry at the end of a winter's trudge and a dull school day, locked out from my home, clutching the pram in one hand, the key in the other, submitting meekly to his remonstrance before he plunged back into the relentless automation – felt then the dreadful urgency of his expectation, his desire to raise me out of his imminent reality; felt above all in myself the absolute absence of anything that could be called a reciprocal ambition; felt only the abiding, impossible, incommunicable sense of loss that seemed to connect me not with him but with the dead, whose literal extinction had placed them beyond any ephemeral embrace.

Five

If only it were possible to ask. Genesis. Exodus. Leviticus. Ecclesiasticus. These are the titles of the books of the Bible. Proper nouns. When we parse sentences we give every part of speech a name. But what do these curious-sounding proper nouns mean? I sneak a look in my dictionary. Genesis is an abstract noun. It means creation. The bibles are open on the desk. Each girl reads a verse or two until at a nod from the teacher the next in the row takes up the story. I return to the homework that is hidden on my knee. Jack throws a stone for Rover. I underline stone in red crayon. Stone is a common noun. But what does stone mean? Stone means only stone. Is it a definition I want, or a description, or a synonym? Rock is not a good synonym. It has a different feel. But what actually does stone mean? Without a stone there in front of my nose in my hand the word seems opaque. I pretend to hold a little cool grey pebble in my hand testing its weight on the palm of my hand. Put that homework away in your desk at once, the teacher shrills. It is impossible to tell her that I have already read the chapter and am bored waiting my turn. To show my indignation I flick roughly through the tissue pages, pretending I cannot find the place. The teacher says crossly: Exodus. What chapter? I mutter. The teacher says: Now Miss Fidget, keep your eyes glued to that page and your hands on that desk.

I was proud of being a good reader but when it was my turn I read in a high, trembling voice, investing in every word, trying to eradicate the misdemeanour by a flawless performance. Afterwards I looked at the teacher for approval, but she was preoccupied, reading. Next, she said. Like a child that cannot read silently without forming the words in her mouth, her lips moved; if there was a halt she instantly supplied the problematic word or intonation, but if she had to say a word that caused a stumble because it was peculiar or suggestive – particularly if it was one that produced a titter like Shittim-wood – her thin-skinned face would flush. After my turn I skipped once more to the end of the chapter and then waited impatiently, not daring to go on reading lest I should lose track altogether and be called on again. Outside, a tree in full leaf grew close to the window, making a deep green shade which was pierced by fine needles of light. If I narrowed my eyes, I could see motes of dust which lazily and slowly danced, until stirred by the lift of a curious hand they moved faster and even faster as the brilliantly lit hand beat the air, then slowly and more slowly as the hand dropped. From far away a voice stammered through the lesson, but I was a prisoner, a slave bound in thongs of sunlight. I breathed out gently and watched the dust dervishes dance to silent music.

It was hot. The tyrant had said he would bring them no more straw to make bricks and yet the tally of work must remain the same. They had gathered straw until their hands bled and their backs were breaking with the strain, their throats parched with the hot dust and with licking the salt sweat from their lips. Slaves. They were mixing straw and dust and water to make bricks that would bake in the sun, and as they worked it was caking in lumps on their hands and feet. They were afraid to sing their songs as they crawled over the burning earth, for if the labour was not enough, there was the lash, made of leather, dried and knotted. But they were not afraid of the tyrant himself because they knew that he was only an instrument of God: in the fullness of time they will be led out of bondage into the wilderness that borders the Red Sea. Glory, glory, glory. Terror and haste. The striped bundles gathered together in the night. The lean brown faces huddled under the hoods. The barefoot children running beside makeshift carts, upon which lurch old men and witless old women. Before them the sea, behind the thunder of hoofs, the rumble of chariot wheels, an army crashing through the scrub, baffled by a false night. But at the water's edge a miracle of light is happening. A wind rushing from the heavens, cleaving the flood. Before them the way lies clear and dry between sheer walls. For a moment they hesitate, appalled by the looming of walls, the great waves held on the upsurge, pulled back by an unnatural planet, before plunging down into the gulf. Behind them the battalions come blundering through the darkness, defeated by the wilderness. With one will the fugitive people leap forward into the chasm, on to the naked sea-bed, a rabble of kinsmen, carts, beasts, laden with cooking vessels and sacred vessels and secret scrolls in boxes of scented wood. When they are safe on the other side the night resumes its normal character, the wind and the light alter. In the dimness they look back and see the barricades burst and break, hurling the bodies, and hear in the quiet air the howling of the barbarian hordes.

If only it were possible to ask. If God is a loving God, I want to ask, how can he murder all these people? I put up my hand. Before I can frame my question, the teacher has pounced. Go, if you must go, she says. I stand to go. I do not need to go but it is easier to comply than to explain that I wanted to ask a question. A girl in the class pipes up: Miss, we are not allowed to go except at break-times. There is a murmur of disapproval from the class: getting other girls into trouble is against the unwritten code. The teacher looks flustered and so snaps at me to sit down again and stop being stupid. The muttering swells and dies down and the reading around the class begins again. Something in me – some resistance – is beginning to swell and harden. To be treated like a small child is bad enough but to be made to look a fool is intolerable. I stare obstinately at one spot on the page, but I cannot sit still. I begin to rummage in my desk and then I slam down my desk lid. The teacher orders me to go and stand outside the door. I go angrily, vowing to myself that I will get my own back on the girl.

At break the teacher tells me to wait by the desk, while the girls file past, some glancing at me with pitying looks, but others gloating. Now, says the teacher, why were you being so silly? This question seems unjust and – to my chagrin – I begin to cry. I cannot remember the last time I cried. Eventually I sob: I only wanted to ask you a question. I see, she says uncertainly, I see. I am bitterly aware that she is wondering whether I am telling the truth. Equally, I also know that most teachers would now inflict some minor punishment in order to end the scene, but that she is completely at a loss. Stalling, she tells me to use my hankie, and, knowing full well that my pockets are empty, I pretend to search in vain until she lifts the flap on her shoulder bag and fishes out her own handkerchief. Suddenly, she smiles and perches herself on the edge of the desk. The last sob turns into a tiny laugh. Crying has released something. Impelled by a sense of injustice – but released by her allowing softness – it comes gabbling out, the whole story: the reading ahead, the waiting, the listening, the asking and the · not-asking, the standing and the sitting down.

Genesis. In the beginning was the Word. Her words are very simple and trusting. Read. Listen. Pay attention. Sit. Do not fidget. Do not try to do your homework at the same time. Then, little by little, you will understand. Then, more briskly: Now, what was the question? I twist her damp, blue-bordered handkerchief round and round my thumb. I say: Is the Bible true? She says gently: The Bible is the word of God. We stand there at the front of the class in the sunlight. She seems unable to end this interview and I cannot let her go because she is the authority; she is in charge of me. I feel rather sorry for her, sorry that I have been inattentive. She is soft. Her pink skin is finely puckered all over and she smells of baby lotion. But something hard in me is determined to have my answer. I persist: But someone must have written it down – on paper. On scrolls, she corrects, holy men wrote down the word of God on scrolls. I look out of the window at the shifting light in the tree. She is still smiling. Still kind. Her lessons are dull because she is too controlling, too nervous to let the class go. Perhaps – even – she is a little slow. She has a habit of hitching her shoulder strap as it slides down the sleeve. I do not want to disturb the peace of this moment, but I cannot stop myself from saying: Suppose they were just ordinary men. To my relief she smiles again and says, happily, because she knows the answer: But the Bible is the living proof of their inspiration.

At last the scripture teacher left the room. A bell rang. It was too late for milk. I rammed my slice of marmalade and bread into my mouth, risking being caught eating in class. Then I went to the desk of the girl who had tried to get me into trouble and scrawled on the lid with chalk: Dorothy Wright is a Pig. At almost fourteen I was far too old for such a piece of childishness and since, in the event, I had not been punished, the action was purely perverse. When the girl came back after break she yanked hold of one of my plaits and a brief scuffle took place. To call it a fight would be an exaggeration. By the time the next teacher arrived we were both red-faced and tousled and everybody was shouting. A desk had been knocked over and ink spilt. As a punishment we were both set to polish desks after school. The teacher kept saying in a shocked voice: Top-form girls do not behave in such a way. I had always been well-behaved at school. But the girl who had picked on me was what we used to call a goody-goody girl, whereas – if being good was being still – for me it was a strain to be good, for restless movement was only the physical manifestation of a mental

73

state: my mind was active. The pacing of the lessons was too slow – not just for me, but for most of the other girls too. One to one it might have been possible for the teachers to teach, but the structure of the school seemed designed to produce inertia. Top-form girls indeed were good learners for they had learned to be more docile than the rest.

Sometimes it seems to me that the regimen prescribed for childhood was a kind of treadmill, devised to tame the creature until it had learned to walk in the accustomed ways. Everything was predetermined. There was no scope for independent action. Home, school, home, school. For years these institutions with all their detailed obligations demanded nothing but passive obedience. In school even ostensible questions were not true questions since only the preferred answer was acceptable. One learned this formula in order to escape notice, and, providing this minimal accord was given, a subterranean life was permitted, which increasingly became the only real source of interest, so that even sitting in a classroom was not all that it appeared. It was as if the lesson – whether it be algebraic formulae or contour maps or Latin conjugations – occupied only the surface of the mind, beneath which a hidden life continued to thrive, scarcely impeded by these superficial engagements, which suffered in consequence from a terrible mediocrity. Teachers seldom seemed able reach this other level. Now and then there were, of course, collisions. A teacher would demand full attention, berating day-dreaming or fidgeting or some other sign of preoccupation, but in a little while after such outbursts the mind would throw off these fetters, retreating back into a contemplative state that was deeply engrossing. And this failure of communication led to a gradual deterioration in the quality of interchanges, which became increasingly typical, shaped more by expectation and inveterate custom than by integral thought. A terrible dullness ensued. And then, in order to survive this mechanical routine, it became necessary to struggle against an overwhelming *ennui*, a powerful negation that felt like a physical condition. My throat began to ache and I began to find it difficult to carry out the simple processes, which ought to have been easy, but which a kind of paralysis of the will made inordinately hard as if being treated like a criminal on a wheel induced a form of mental aberration.

And this condition was widespread, since of all these supposedly capable girls that began to droop and sicken, I came to be amongst the survivors, those who were not cleverer or more sturdy but simply more conforming than the rest. As intellectual beings we were dying of boredom. In the evenings, the preparation we were given to do for school seemed to consist of an endless series of repeated operations, and the effort of concentration needed in order to respond to this spur to ambition became greater and greater, while the content of the exercises seemed less and less meaningful. The bouts of paralysis increased in frequency and length, which meant that every piece of school work was executived heroically in the face of inertia at a minimal level of competence. In my case, only my fear of my father's reaction to outright failure – my knowledge that success at school was my only hope, in his eyes, of a better future – guaranteed even this average standard.

My parents believed in education not in itself but as an agent of self-improvement which must eventually take material form. More-over, if her belief was partly mystical, connected tenuously of course, but indissolubly, with side-plates, fish knives and forks, lace doilies, he was a shrewd man who knew the market value of the common subjects. Mathematics – by its association, I suppose, with money – he rated highest. He wanted me to excel in some field that would guarantee a good income. In this respect he was unusual: few people I ever knew had such expectations for their daughters. But then, he had no sons. To be a teacher would be adequate and safe, but he had a preference for other professions – medicine, law. And because I had no aptitude in science and no idea how to translate his aspirations into practical expedients and was too timid to ask teachers, I was paradoxically spurred on by him to achieve the status of an autonomous individual – a rare thing for a girl of my background – and yet doomed in advance to fall short of his highest expectations. I never would become a doctor, a lawyer, a dentist, or an accountant. His notion of worldly success demanded automatic progress along a well-marked route. But to me all was hazy. Above all, I was already wayward, divided, confused and undermined before the stakes were drawn.

Exodus. A going out. A departure or migration. Was that the day when I began finally to suspect that God had no existence outside the mind? For if these were indeed ordinary men touched by the sacred fire we had only their testimony that the tongues were indeed of God. Out of the window across the school field there was a young maple tree in new leaf, rippling in the wind like a small pale flame. Suppose the burning bush was only a yellow blossom tree? Suppose – passed by word of mouth from ear to ear down the long ages like a game of whispers – it had all happened long ago and – unembellished by time – was only a grim plod through a barren land, that enchanted flight? But if there was no other form of life, there was no after life, no God, no Holy Ghost, no ghosts. This thought was pleasing. At night I had always been afraid of seeing something supernatural. At first it was very reassuring to think that the danger was only in the mind. But it was still a real danger. For even if there was nothing lurking at the corner of the stair, the mind could not entirely be trusted not to invent some horror. In the hall at home where we kept our outdoor clothes in an old wardrobe, it was a test of courage to stand in the dark and look up the stairs. If the box-room door was open, the faint green gas-glow from the street lamp was now and then intensified by the passing headlamps of a rare car, which fled across the wall at the head of the stair. How easy it would be to mistake this fleeting light for a spirit form! Once in the snow I had found a frozen fur glove and a cold hand clutched my heart: I had imagined it was a dead rat. How easy it would be to be deluded by these transparent illusions upon the wall.

But why if there were no supernatural forces did the fear persist? My mother and I were both so frightened of the dark that when we were alone in the house and listening to an exciting play on the radio we dared not go upstairs, and used – secretly – to pass water in a bucket in the kitchen. I wanted a rational explanation for everything. My mother was fond of telling the story of how during the war when she was coming home late from work one night she had asked a policeman to walk with her up the dark street in the black-out. And how when – alerted by something in his manner – they reached the door and she had hurriedly got her key in the lock and then herself over the threshold, he had tried to force his way into the house. And she had cried in a great loud voice, though it was not true: My sister is here. Another time she had come home and found a thief had tried to cut a hole with a diamond in a window-pane just beside the catch. Afterwards her youngest sister had come to keep her company in the war while my grandmother was away, and they had gone dancing together and had the house all to themselves. And one day a neighbour that she never talked to again said hintingly: While the cat's away the mice play.

One evening a man was working at the house. My parents were both out and my sister was sleeping. I was doing my homework in my dressing-gown. It was summer and the neck was open; the stuff was thin, quite loosely woven, and I had outgrown the size a little. I worked with a pencil in rough before making a fair copy in ink, and when I came to unscrew the bottle in order to fill the fountain pen I found the cap was stuck. In any case, I wanted to attract the man's attention. I was going to make a drink. He was a little friendly man, half a head shorter than I, one of those sprightly bullet-headed men, always cracking his knuckles, joking and teasing, a man who worked as a brick-layer, whose hands were hard and rough as if the mortar had settled in his skin, whose face was grainy, weathered and scarred, roughly shaven with gingery stubble on his chin that glinted like specks of mica. My father was passionately property conscious, and perhaps because he alone of all our numerous family owned his own house, he was forever getting jobs done on the cheap to preserve the fabric – cleaning the gutterings, pointing, slating, coating the bricks with an impermeable substance that was guaranteed to keep out the damp and seal the cement in its pristine condition. It was non-union labour, eked out over months so that each visit cost only a few shillings – baccy for the man and not too great a burden for the family purse. And because these transactions were part favour, part financial, my mother always felt an element of obligation, made the man high teas, rashers of best bacon, two eggs, apple pie, madeira cake, extravagantly strong tea, treated him with the condescension due to a decent character, who, according to her finely distinguished gradings, belonged a little lower than herself down the social scale and therefore must be accorded a distant but scrupulous kindness. She never used his first name but always called him mister. Taking my cue from her, I fussed him, as a visitor, but also I took it upon myself to cancel out her coolness, which seemed to me to err on the side of snobbery. At home everybody praised me for being domesticated as well as studious, and because I could never get enough admiration I made excessive efforts to charm, laying out his supper tray, cutting his sandwiches diagonally, whipping the milk in the pan so that a light foam appeared on the brimming cup, in imitation of the espresso coffee which was just then becoming fashionable in coffee bars.

Beneath this legitimate cosseting lay the desire to make this man notice me as a woman. He was outside on a ladder. I went to the door and called him, holding up the bottle of ink. He came indoors. Instead

77

of taking the bottle from me, he grasped my hand inside his own large hand, and, keeping the ink steady, he unscrewed the top with his other hand. I thanked him and tried to remove my hand, but all of a sudden, not letting go, he grabbed hold of my shoulder. There was no mistaking his intention, yet I pretended to misunderstand in order to avoid an embarrassing scene. I took a backward step up the stairs, laughing light-heartedly, as if he was making a joke. I was too flustered to read his face. I cried out: Be careful not to get ink on the carpet. Somehow I pulled away, freeing myself, and stumbled up the stairs to the landing, but he followed, almost falling over me in his determination to catch hold of me again, his head bumping into my neck. I gave him a violent push, and because he was off balance, he fell – half-fell, half-staggered – down the stairs. Instantly, without waiting to see what had happened to him, I ran to the room in which my sister slept and dragged her bed a few inches to jam the door. I heard my name called once, then silence.

After this incident, which frightened me a good deal, I was very angry with the man. I told nobody at first, partly out of embarrassment, and partly out of the knowledge that my own manner had been provocative. I had wanted the man to be charmed, but I had not expected him to transgress the boundaries set there in my defence – by courtesy because he had been accepted within the family, and by custom because I thought of myself as still a child, and by convention because he was a man with a wife and children of his own. I was frightened by the urgency of his behaviour, which, though it did not go very far, had more in it of the spirit of an attack than an embrace. Above all, I see now, I was frightened because this episode, slight in itself, struck a chord, evoking three or four moments in consciousness that had not yet shaped themselves into a connection, and which – even then – did not make sense. Thus, at the time I cannot recall articulating these memories of earlier assaults, but the panic that suffused me that evening after the confrontation on the stairs was akin to the other states, when – externally more passive, younger, less immune – I was subjected to a sudden rupturing of that taboo against the unlawful touching of children that normally encloses them within an invisible armour.

In the days after the incident on the stairs I wondered what the man would do or say next. The thought of meeting him by accident in the street was enough to set my heart beating fast. What if he made an approach? How would it be proper for me to behave? Part of me wanted to punish him by creating a fuss, but the part of me that felt responsible wanted to keep it private. It was as if I had aroused the man's attention deliberately out of my vanity and thus caused the disequilibrium that followed. I had been testing my own power. In reality I was angry with myself for inaugurating this episode. For this reason I did not tell my parents what had happened, pretending to myself that I preferred simply to let the situation die away of its own accord. But when, the following weekend, he came with the tools of his trade and jauntily set up his ladder, when my mother spread her best cloth and instructed me to call him for his tea, the temptation to seek revenge was too great. I was churlish at the table and my mother chid me in front of his face, making excuses for me, while he, cloddish, unshaven, smeared with cement, sat there stolidly, stuffing himself with our food. My mother was displeased with me, and afterwards, eager to exonerate myself, I said: Well, I don't care if I was rude because he was rude to me the other night.

At first, she looked panic-stricken. She made me repeat the details several times, and only when she was satisfied that nothing serious had happened to me did she say: On no account mention it to your father. At the time I took her word for it that it would cause a great uproar if I were to do so, and that my father would probably horse-whip the man – a quaint archaism, since horse-riding had just about disappeared from our urban scene, and meant more to instil in me the dramatic nature of the consequences if I were to babble than to suggest an actual affray. Indeed, it seemed to me later that she was aware that if my father were to be informed, his position would be awkward, since he would almost certainly have recoiled from any such action. I think my mother must have known that the knowledge would burden my father and that he would be unable to act at all. Her instinct was to avoid exaggeration. Moreover, she detected in my own story and in my behaviour those elements of provocation of which I was myself aware. Together, as we tidied the kitchen, the man still outside at work, we mulled over the subject, until she concluded: You egged him on, whereas a proper woman – a lady – should show more reserve.

If gradually my mother and I grew apart, it seems to me now that it was mainly because her standards for my conduct forced me into hypocrisy. Everybody called my mother a lady. In the streets sometimes people stopped me and said: You have got a lovely mother.

The very qualities that within the home made her less of a force – her gentleness and self-effacement – were highly regarded by others, to whom she appeared refined and considerate, so that at work, little by little over the years, she gained in status and assurance. She had begun her working life as an order-seeker, a kind of messenger girl in the factory, and some twenty years later she would finally work herself into the position of employment officer, a progress that was unusual in those days, and that testified to her perseverance, her tact, her adaptability, her powers of conciliation. At this time, though, she had become a clerk, and her aspirations were still vague, almost romantic: a garden, a table under a fringed parasol, taking tea in an afternoon dress. Yet she was a sensible woman. She had no inclination to injure the man who tried to force himself on me; she simply ensured that he was phased out of our domestic arrangements. My father's queries were parried and a new person was found to do jobs, while I was warned to keep my distance. But it was this temperate conduct, this smoothing over of all points of conflict, that in the end prevented open discourse, because when I drew the man's attention I was driven by some kind of inner compulsion, but my mother thought that flirting was merely unlady-like. According to her code, such display, such blatant offering of the self, was wrong; and yet, for me, the need to assert that self was absolutely imperative. And because she was so proper, so perfectly controlled, I had to feign indifference in order to seem correct. Ostensibly the closest of friends, we were not close at all.

Every Sunday morning we went to church together while my father watched the dinner in the oven. For this reason we always ate stew on Sunday because it was the easiest thing. In the afternoon I was now a Sunday school teacher. My mother had no idea that the boy at church was the real reason for these devotions because, at the very time when my father was still strong in my eyes, it became necessary for me to be disobedient. Even though I knew that for me – with my destiny as a scholarship girl – to take up with a boyfriend was absolutely forbidden, the fantasy figure ceased to be an acceptable substitute. I began to signal. I became conniving. I insinuated the idea of a birthday party into my mother's mind. She loved the idea of special occasions. One day she brought home five little deckle-edged invitation cards. My six guests would include one of my cousins. Somehow I managed to get *his* name on the list. I handed him the invitation at church. At close quarters his eyes were a very dark blue. If I let my eyes linger on his face for long enough I knew he was getting the message. Somehow, wordlessly, we had reached a secret understanding. Though we went nowhere it was rumoured amongst the other children at church that we were going out together. My mother – seemingly unaware of this sub-text – was very kind and playful; the preparations, the lists, the games, all of these matters she entered into with child-like earnestness. She took the best tea-set out of the china cabinet and washed it in soap-flakes to make it shine, and polished it with one of her best tea-cloths, hem-stitched by hand out of Irish linen squares – six place settings matched, so that there could only be six members of the party, though on family occasions when the aunts clubbed in and brought their stuff we might be much more numerous. My party was patterned with a tissue of fine rituals – buffing teaspoons, purchasing cube sugar, folding paper napkins – which invested existence with a sense of gracious living. I wore my confirmation outfit, a white voile blouse and a blue skirt, and my mother patted my cheeks with rouge. She had made sandwiches and jelly and a cake. And after tea, he and I, and the cousin, the girl-friend from school and a girl-friend from church and a neighbour's child that my mother felt sorry for because – she said – they did not get much, played table tennis and Lotto and consequences. And made difficult conversation.

A few days after the party – it was the Easter holidays – I took my sister for a walk in the push-chair and went past his street several times. He had a little sister of his own who was playing in their yard, and she fetched him out and the two of them came with us for a walk, me pushing the chair that my sister had really outgrown, the two little girls running ahead, the two of us walking along, a yard apart, speechless with embarrassment.

It was a very cold day. We came to some waste ground where the clay path was like moulded iron. He was thin and not warmly dressed, his face very sculptured and cold-looking in the March frost. On the cheek nearest me there was a tiny scar. Not to touch was intolerable. It had to be made flesh. My heart began to race as I slipped my hand out of my school glove and with one finger very gently stroked his cheek. I made a question of my face to justify this assault. He said proudly: Shaving. My heart hammered. I could not look him in the eye. There were some miserable thorn bushes beside the path with a few blackened berries. With my bare hand I broke off a twig and gave it to him in his hand, inviting him silently to take it as a token. I was passionately in love. We walked hand in hand, speechless with joy.

On Sunday evening after church, we tried to kiss, our faces colliding. We clung together, pressing lips against lips. His chest felt hard and bony. I could feel his ribs, the buttons of his coat, his teeth. The kiss took away my breath. The street reeled. Then I broke free and galloped down the street to my own gate. I stood a minute before I let the hinge creak. My legs were weak. I heard a clatter and looked back. He had found a tin can in the gutter and was dribbling it along the ground as he trotted off towards his own street. It seemed a very boyish thing to do at that exalted moment and my feeling for him was abruptly extinguished like a weak flame blown out by a gust of cold air.

Living in the wake of this grand illusion – for within a few days I had determined that romantic love was a phantom – I was deeply troubled by my own inconsistency. Now I could see that he was just an ordinary boy. Whenever he came in sight I looked the other way, and before long it was as if we had never known each other at all. In every great novel I had read that no good woman was capable of fickleness. I felt empty and disappointed. There was a great lack left where this obsession had held sway for so long. Gradually I began to drift more into the space where I seemed to lie becalmed, alone. The inertia that at first belonged only to school tasks became more general and pervasive, like a progressive illness that leads to an aggravated melancholy. At my centre, where I lived, there was a nullity. In some horrible way – not articulated but experienced none the less – it felt to me as if I was suppressing symptoms, which, if revealed, would elicit at best sympathy, at worst a shocked aquiescence, and this produced a hysterical desire to confide together with a terrified and obstinate pursuit of privacy. At other times, I simply seemed to have lost my centre of gravity and my support and to be in extreme danger of spilling out without my will, without my own volition into the great, the endless void.

Everything was changing all the time. One day thick white lines were painted on the road at the bottom of the street and Belisha beacons appeared. Another day two shops were knocked together and a petrol pump was erected on the pavement outside. Then somebody had a telephone installed and wires were looped across the street. As a child I had imagined that the world in which I found myself was fixed. To me the grown people were like totem poles. Everything was absolute. There was an obscure, unreasoned reason in everything which impinged upon my senses as pure sensation undiluted by thought. The kitchen was a warm brown blur. A draught that stirs the air as a door opens. A gurgle as water ran down the plug-hole tickling my toes. During this time of inward and outward change, something in me wanted to close my eyes and be lulled to sleep, not to see. And yet much of the time I felt stifled because something else wanted to be free.

That summer we went on holiday to Blackpool. We stayed in a house on the north shore, where the gardens were full of huge hydrangeas. Early each morning, even when the weather was wild and rainy, my father took me to swim in the sea while my mother went out to buy food which was cooked by the landlady. We ate on our best behaviour in a dining room that smelled of rancid butter. When it was fine we sat on the sands and when it was dull we took long walks along the long featureless shore. On the nights when there was racing, my father went to the local dog-track while my mother and I stayed out of doors till twilight and then crept indoors and sat in the room and were served biscuits and tea before bed. On the other evenings we went to the variety shows. Best of all there was dancing in the Tower ballroom when my father alternated between whirling my mother about the floor and painstakingly teaching me the steps. And sometimes, to my intense gratification, a boy or even a man would come and ask me to dance. I loved to dance. I loved the music of the popular songs, loved the words, the endlessly repeated variations of the same theme: love me, love me, love me. Always it seemed as if music had fingers that could get inside and squeeze the heart with joy.

One afternoon, dragging my sister along with me for an alibi, I went to find the old house. I remembered the name of the street. For some reason I felt I must keep this pilgrimage a secret. It was the height of the season and the promenade was thronged. Now and then a string of prancing singing youths, their arms interlaced, barred our way. But the mood was good-humoured. It was like going into town on a Saturday afternoon when everybody was on a spending spree, that reckless feeling of work-people released from their bondage, scouring the golden mile in search of pleasure. My sister kept complaining that her sandals were hurting, but I bought candy-floss to keep her quiet, and when the soft pink substance left a burning on the tongue she cried and had to be carried. Eventually we came to the street, but nothing seemed the same. There was the divide in the terrace, the house with the open door, but I dared not knock on the door. I wanted to say: Here I am back again just as I used to be. Adrift, I kept hold of my sister's hand as she tried to escape. I stood at the cross-roads and stared. There was no public house, no ice-cream parlour, no café round the corner with lace curtains tied in bows. Disappointed, I trailed my sister back to our lodgings, bribing her with piggy-backs most of the way. At tea-time, afraid that she would unwittingly betray me, I confessed: I went for a walk to see where we used to stay, Grandma and me. My mother gave me a warning look. My father said sharply: What was that? Stayed where? Silly girl, my mother said, it was just a week. Just one week a long time ago in the war.

The following morning when I got out of bed I found a tiny smear of blood on the sheet. I pulled up the covers to hide the spot. I felt sticky. I swivelled my night-gown round but there was no stain because as usual it had ridden up my body in the night. I stood still, not knowing whether to expect a flood or a trickle. When nothing happened, I went to the bathroom, tore off two pieces of toilet paper and dabbed at myself cautiously to confirm the situation. Stiff-legged, I went back to the bedroom where my sister was still asleep. Afraid to sit down or dress, I propped myself on my elbows and looked out of the window: in the back garden of the boarding house there were rows of lettuces and beans and a tethered dog. In a while my father would tap at the door to see if I was ready to go swimming. What should I say? During swimming lessons at school I would have to sit on the bench, and when the teacher came along the row with the register I would have to say: Excused. Perhaps I should say to my father: I'm not well. But I didn't feel ill at all; except for an extreme reluctance to mention the matter, I felt quite ordinary. After a while my mother came into the bedroom with clean clothes for my sister. She said: You should never stand on a strange carpet in bare feet. Irritated, I pulled back the covers and pointed to the sheet. Have you got a pain? she said. I shook my head. What about the mess? Never mind, she said, we can soak that little mark in the sink. I could feel tears beginning to well up in my eyes. I turned back to the window. The blurred dog was very fat and old-looking; it walked wearily along the path as far as the rope would let it go and then flopped down in the dust on its belly. Why did you tell a lie? I said. My mother was stripping off the sheet. It was ages and ages, I said, weeks and weeks at least – every summer in the war. He was a long way away, my mother breathed, and he thought the world of you. So? It was best for him to believe we were all together in our own little house. So? It would have grieved him to know how hard we had to struggle to keep things together. I closed my eyes, willing myself not to cry. Don't worry about the sheet, she said very softly, it will all come out in the wash. The longing to gather it all together and tell my mother was almost unbearable. But what could I say? Where could I begin? My sister was bouncing on the bed. I said: There's a roly-poly dog sleeping in the yard. Let me see, she cried, let me see. Hugging her hard, I held her against the window-sill, until she wriggled to get free.

Six

Making sense out of those evanescent years is like writing in water: as long as I am still here the substance is constant, but the meaning eludes, changing from moment to moment as the lines form and instantly dissolve, while light glances across the vanishing wake and not quite catches the shape. A liquid art. My memory discloses dappled water, myself a girl squinting into the sunshine, my legs lifted to the shimmering brink, where bright flakes wink and shift, myself drifting, bemused, enthralled. I lie there, thinking: these moments are like drops of water. Thinking: impossible to keep hold of these moments. These droplets. Water. A glass of water at nose-height on the kitchen window-sill in which somebody has sprinkled two or three tiny circles of pink paper that swell into lotus blossoms. My nose touches the glass. My finger sneaks into the water. See-through. The same yet not the same. The glass is see-through like water but solid. But in winter-time the cold will make icicles under the eaves and fern patterns on the window-panes. Water is ice and vapour. Or should I say frost and mist? I must engrave these words on my memory. I repeat: blue-green water. Aquamarine. Aqueous tints. Blue-green water on blue-white skin that is cool and rubbery to the touch. I am lying in a pool in a public park amidst the pretty litter of a summer afternoon – cricket, pastel frocks, a blaze of salvias – while the realisation that meaning is arbitrary presents itself, on this brilliant day, as a dark portent. I lift my fingers from the water, which drips softly, finding its own level, a material absolute. I see the wet skin, pink, wrinkled, faintly chlorinated, apart. I realise my own separateness from the water, from the green-painted cubicle doors, the blue-tiled tank, the damp, trodden grass, the basking bodies, my own legs and arms and trunk and head. And yet I am part of it all. I am my pale trailing members, my bloodless fingernails, my teeth, my hair. I pull through the water, my heart pumping steadily, and oxygen bubbles out of my mouth and nose and is taken in again from the air. This process goes on without my volition. Is ordinary. Yet between my very self and these objects a crack appears that rapidly presents itself as an immense crevasse, a vast abyss. It is all a question of proportion and relationships. The light breeds a kind of terror. My head is prolific: it creates barriers. I am a floating island. Nobody else in the world knows there are Japanese flowers floating in a glass of water on the window-sill. I begin to experience a continual longing for some antidote to this appalling solitude, an antidote for which the only name I know is love. Moreover, as I lie there, splayed in the water, watching, bumped now and then by the bodies of other bathers, I become aware that I am watching at that very moment now, and now, for the arrival that will release me from my own absence, that I am asking the question: is he the one, or he, or he?

My father also swims, but he simply lowers himself into the water at the shallow end and with a heavy wallowing stroke goes backwards and forwards from one end to the other, taking exercise, while my mother sits near the paddling pool to watch my sister play with our little cousins and friends. Each aunt has two children younger than I. On fine Sundays after church the whole family goes to the park. We take a picnic and spend all day in the open air as long as the sun lasts. Sometimes, if there is a cricket match, we spread out our blanket on the hill-side overlooking the green and hire deck-chairs from the cricket pavilion. I am too old to play, too young to be allowed the luxury of a deck-chair. I lie on my stomach, reading. When it gets uncomfortable I roll over on my back and hold the book up over my face. I prop myself first on one elbow, then the other. There is a constant buzz of conversation. The men talk about racing and politics. The women also talk politics but at the same time they knit and dispense food which is packed in biscuit tins and grease-proof paper. Now and then I am dispatched to fetch ice-creams. When the little children begin to get restive I have to organise games or take them for a walk. Sometimes I continue to read as I am strolling along, and this is only partly because I am bookish. In part it is because reading gives me a pretext to detach myself. Too much is coming in all the time. Everything is streaming in all the time like light, blinding. Blinkered and protected by the book I am able to shut out the huge spaces of the park, which is so full of everything I cannot understand. Even cricket is redolent with mysteries. What is a maiden over? The slips? Silly mid-on? Instead of asking, I drift away from these cross-currents of meaning. I lie face-down on the grass. Each blade is distinct, sprouting up out of fibrous shoots. I tug, but the roots do not yield. The dirt is hard like baked clay. Water. Earth. Air. These are the elements. And fire. But why fire? Everything has evolved out of these ingredients. But there must be a beginning. I lie on my back and look up into the sky. If there is no beginning and no end? A shiny beetle, the size of a pin-head, gun-metal green, crawls on my arm, hesitating as it reaches the crook of my elbow, and then scurrying on down the long trail to my wrist. If I press its little life out between my finger and thumb it will leave a tiny smear of blood. I give it a flick and it drops into the turf. How long will it last? How tall does it see the great stems of the grass? How is it possible for this teeming world, this universe, these vast immensities, to creep inside my head?

The district was poor. Both our church and our church hall stood on tracts of rough ground that had never been properly landscaped, and this gave to their environs a somewhat wild and threatening aspect. The site probably included some two or three acres that formed a kind of no-man's land between the private terraced housing of the kind where I lived and which was mostly landlord owned, and thus rented, but quite respectable, and an immense council estate, that was itself supposed to be a dangerous place, full of families that kept coal in the bath and beat their children. In this borderland the church and hall were surrounded by shaggy, untended ground in which grew elder-berry, bramble, grass, wild rhubarb, partly but not entirely concealing a variety of waste building material, broken sewage pipes and the like, as well as old mattresses, rusting pushchairs, the charred remains of burnt furniture, the rotting detritus of moonlight flits and house purges surreptitiously dumped over the sagging wire fence by non-church-going parishioners and now and then cleared out by earnest church youths superintended by indignant church wardens.

The church itself was a modest edifice with no decorative features inside or out, a modern building of purplish grey brick with clear glass windows. It must have been designed to be in keeping with the council estate, and it shared the same air of bleak neglect; and yet, during the dim evenings, its barn-like interior could evoke a certain mystery, a hush, a hint of infinitude. The church hall had once belonged to the army: a left-over from the war, it was quite simply a decayed Nissen hut, long and narrow with an improvised board stage at one end across which were looped drunkenly some old black-out curtains. Behind this stage was a kitchen and a couple of lavatories, and a number of cupboards in which were stored youth club apparatus – the table tennis nets, and bats, and balls; bits of felt and wools and silks for an embroidery class that never got started; thick white pots for use on social evenings; a first-aid box and a fire extinguisher; and three bell tents used by the guides and scouts. Everything was always grimed with dust. Every time there was a church dance, the floor was liberally sprinkled with French chalk to counteract its lumps and splinters, but mainly the dust was simply the dried out residue of the muddy ground outside, for there was only a cinder path to the church hall and when it rained the access was filthy as the water drained into the channel round the shed. Everything was cheap and poor, for money was in short supply and with everybody in full employment there was hardly sufficient time for the project of clearing the land that was always being proposed; nor was there any person of sufficient energy or power to authorise such an enterprise. Women who worked long hours for small wages could undertake the regular calendar of events – lace runners and pots of pickles for the autumn fair – but not heavy labour. The vicar himself did nothing to raise funds; nor did he appear except briefly at these social functions. He was a supposed mystic surrounded by ineffectual persons of vague goodwill – my mother amongst them – who, having nothing to donate except their brief leisure hours, ran the various clubs and societies and raised funds for absolute necessities.

But at night, when the crêpe-clad lights burned with a dull red glow and music pulsed softly behind thick, dusty curtains spangled with tinsel moons, there was a magic in the atmosphere of the hall that seemed to call to us as we picked our way in our best heels between the muddy puddles. This was our social centre. My mother and I dressed for these outings with the most ardent attention to each exquisite detail. Will this rouge do, she would demand, or is it too orange? For my father and my older aunts the very idea of make-up was associated with impropriety, and so the improvement had to be imperceptible. And which brooch goes best with the donkey-brown jumper, she would ponder, the marcasite or the cultured pearl?

That winter I had a Scots kilt. My aunt taught me to knit lacy patterns and I made myself a jumper in angora wool with a design like fine cobwebs that revealed the straps of my brassière. I licked red sweet papers and rubbed the dye on my lips. My mother dabbed perfume behind my ears and on my wrists and lent me a pair of her best nylons. I kept raising my legs to check the seams, hoping people would notice. The little rubber knobs on the back of the suspenders pressed into my thighs when I forgot and put my elbows on my knees to prop up my head as I was in the habit of doing; my mother frowned at me sometimes, and lowered her eyes discreetly to my lap, which meant I should cross my legs or keep them together. When I gazed at myself in my mother's dressing-table mirror with its swinging wings that gave me image after image down the long glassy corridors, I asked: Am I beautiful? If I drooped my eyelids provocatively and peeped through the fringes of my lashes I could see rainbow lights. But was I entrancing? Would this be the evening when the perfect person materialised? Would he recognise my beauty? At the supreme moment of recognition what would he say? What would he do? Whatever shall I say? What shall I do? How will it be possible for us to come together? Or to be alone? Knowing that the scrubby land behind the church with its dips and hollows, its improvised shacks made out of cardboard boxes and old bed-ends, was a kind of shanty town, where the older children, not the church children, but the others, conducted their forbidden trysts, their experiments with cigarettes and camp-fires, their wrestling matches and gang fights, their looks and feels, their squealing encounters, writhings, silent clinchings, witnessed with appalled fascination in glimpses along the hurried path. An impossible direction. The gulf between such meetings and my dreams was impassable. If a tin can kicked along an alley was enough to shatter the fragile shell of my desire, it would never be possible for me to enter that forbidden world and share that secret knowledge.

My aunt turned me round and round by the shoulder, examining me for faults, slipped stitches. My mother giggled, simpering: Does it show too much, Agnes? I looked at myself in the kitchen mirror, seeing the white, silky shapes under the blue cobwebs. My aunt, deeply modest, coloured and pursed her lips. She's only a bairn, she said sharply. Bairn was not a local term, but a word my mother's elder sisters had brought with them from the mining village near Sheffield; a mark of their distinction, almost an affectation of country goodness. Then, relenting, she said: She's getting to be a bonny lass. I loved my aunt. I thanked her for helping me and she drew me towards her and gave me a hug. Her body was heavy, solid and corseted, smelling – like my grandmother – of lavender. She made my mother seem flighty and highly strung, and yet it was my mother who was making her way in the factory – had gone from taking messages to clerking after the war and had already been given a rise and put over another girl – whereas my aunt· was only a cleaning lady in a shoe-shop down the road. But I never doubted that my aunt was the boss in her house; and this serene assumption of authority that indicated not a passion for power but simply a state of knowing best was always comforting. Her daughter had died, then her husband, but she had survived and had another husband who, in contrast to my father, seemed gentle and friendly. He read library books and sometimes told me a good title. Bonny. I hugged myself. But her choice of word was worrying. The connotations were troublesome. It could mean pretty, but it had a sense also of well-built, strong, wholesome. These were the very qualities my aunt would commend. And that was discouraging. A heroine should not be robust. Out of my reading I had constructed a quite precise model in which small feet, fine bones, white slender hands, delicate mouldings of a substance more refined and tempered than mere flesh, transparent skin, hair like spun glass, eyes whose calm gaze implied transcendence, all conspired to deny ordinary animal well-being. And already then, whatever my own actual physical condition, a spiritual quality – complicated, febrile, searching – had taken possession of me, though as yet it remained unrecognised by myself.

Weeks pass again, breaking the thread. What stopped the compulsion there? Interruptions, always interruptions. My aunt turned me round and round by the shoulder. And there it stopped. I want to hurry back to that moment. I want to be direct. But there is a residual shame in me at the thought of selfhood and all that it implies – a feeling that I ought to be complying with that selfless ideal, whose spirit guided my girlhood through to its inevitable extinction. For those women of my family simply lived for the family; even when they worked – and intermittently, of necessity, they all worked outside their homes – their great consuming interest was the family. Thus my aunt turns me round and round by the shoulder: I long to be admired and loved and she does love me – she gives me a playful pat and I smell her warm, clean lavender smell – but I am also being measured. To satisfy her standard

I must look decent. As I comb out my plaits and make my hair into a pony-tail, I suddenly think of a dray-horse with big, strong ankles plodding along, its head steadily lifting and falling between its broad shoulders. I toss my head, once to try out the pony-tail and once because it seems more heroic to be mettlesome. My aunt gives me a cross little push and says: You're a bag of nerves, just like your mother. I pirouette so that my skirt becomes a rainbow umbrella. She wants me to be a patient work-horse. And she says, as I sneak another look in the glass: Now mind you watch yourself. I know what this means. It means I must keep my legs crossed and not go getting into trouble. For always on the fringes of our lives – as in the literature – there have been girls in trouble. But whereas in books such girls were destined to die or suffer intolerable humiliations, the girls in our streets eventually emerged through belated unions into a state of decency.

Again a lapse. Always these interruptions. On a simply practical level this is why it is hard for any woman to adopt a purpose and carry it through with rigour. These distractions constantly devour my attention. I am being eaten alive, carried away in minute fragments by batches of sandwiches, bundles of socks, rugby shirts, familial disputes. Somehow again I have lost sight of myself. I have become disengaged from my real intention.

This making is my real work, but the other – the home-making – is also rooted in the space at the centre of myself, so that when I come back – when, after weeks and weeks of other-life, I come to these pages and try to put edge to edge – I find myself displaced again; and often this dislocation leads to a loss of confidence, a flagging will, a fatal weakness in me that must not be allowed to win. And so I persevere. Or risk the rift. I feel myself being drawn towards the drowning edge. This is the same self that lies in the water, discovering that desire is more potent than disillusionment, wondering: Is he the one, or he, or he?

An October afternoon. The church hall dimly lit, twilight outside, waste ground, tumbled weeds, old man's beard rambling over scrubby land, sorrel dried out to the hue of auburn hair, wire netting rotting in rusting festoons. Within, the ladies of the autumn bazaar stacked away the trestles and swept the floor. Dust veiled the atmosphere. In the evening there was to be a dance – a man with a radiogram importantly rigged up his gear. Thick black cable snaked across the stage to a junction box, where another man tinkered with electric wires. Nobody wanted to go home in the interim because our togetherness created a sense of possibility, an excitement. Girls giggled, while a knot of small boys wrestled in the back porch, tangled, clumsily scrimmaging back and forth, all arms and legs and grubby flannel shorts. Then the table tennis equipment was fetched out from a cupboard under the stage and the ping-pong ball was skipping across the threadbare green baize over the taut green net. The girls watched. Few of the girls ever played. At home sometimes we fixed a net over the kitchen table and played a diminutive version. My mother was a nifty player, swift, alert, keen to win. But in public it would have seemed forward to take part. The very thought of standing up and demanding a bat made my cheeks burn, my heart beat dreadfully fast, and yet watching, the passive part, enforced a nervous concentration, a hothouse quality that drove us to subversion, sniggering and preening: there was nothing to do and we needed to be doing. The room was ready for evening. We had already been permitted to put out the cups and saucers, to cut the triangular sandwiches and arrange the iced buns under clean cloths borrowed from home to keep off the dust till the proper time. A record played syncopated music, a jazzy piano, a catchy tune, peculiarly nostalgic, tuning us into some other realm where sunlit streets, shutters, shuffling black servants evoked an alien, filmic glamour.

I was sitting on a long wooden bench against a wooden wall, suspended in this medium, these disparate impressions, precise images, inchoate emotions. It was warm, dusty, itchy. Suddenly my heart expanded, aching. I wanted to run, to move with the music, to shake off the lassitude, to escape from the pressure of mere being, to achieve some kind of release. At the table tennis table, a boy laughed – a sudden gruff explosion. Inside me, in the pit of my body, I experienced a convulsion. I must have stood, impelled involuntarily towards the voice, the sudden, deep-throated laughter, because almost at once I remember bumping down on to the hard seat, drawing myself downwards and inwards, hugging myself to myself to still that unfamiliar pulsation. It was as if my body had tried to open, and then, as abruptly, clenched shut again. I thought: I need to go. I might have called it toilet because that was the refined word: to my shame some of my elderly relatives would still call it the closet. But almost at once the sensation passed away, leaving behind a residue of curiosity. I stared at the boy with the laugh, and, listening, realised that his voice had broken and that the sound that had unlocked this sudden feeling was that brazen timbre, oddly off-key, a call to that further physical experience that was forbidden. I said something to another girl and laughed, a high, silly laugh, wanting to be noticed, and the boy coloured, missed his shot, and ran towards me for the ball, which I held out in a closed hand, deliberately teasing, withholding, till our fingers touched and his eyes were forced to meet my timid, deliberate stare. My aunt had pulled me round to face her face and looked me sternly in the eyes: Now then, she said, you want to watch yourself.

And the question, in the den, in the long ardent walks during the later years of girlhood, in the leisure hours that became more and more available as instruction became more concise and periods of private study were extended, the question recurring throughout these years with the inevitability of a compulsion was partly at least a simple: how? How? Because though the necessity of coupling was understood both as a physical and a social act, the mechanics of the business were inexplicable in the absence of precise fact. How – physically – could such a connection be achieved? How – socially – could it be tolerated, when the very notion even of private nakedness produced a burning shame?

So that in the church hall I sat, watching the boy with the deep laugh – his face, squarish, ruddy, uncouth, genial – watching, puzzled, fascinated, half-repelled, while my body played tricks, opening and shutting under the pleated plaid skirt like one of those dark sea-anemones viewed dimly, mysteriously, in the shallow pools at the seaside where the standing water is warm to the touch and the sand, richly laden with glittering fragments, flows between the seeking fingers like soft silt.

The room in which I work now has a large window which overlooks a secluded park. I spend hours gazing, making this scene my own: the encircling hills, then the screen of trees and shrubs, some irregular stretches of lawn, two large beds full of rose bushes with bronze leaves. At the road's edge – the road itself is not visible – a stream is disgorged by a culvert which runs under a wild patch in the park. Elderberry flourishes here, and wild rhubarb flaunting huge leaves and great heads of hemlock. I remember the smell of rain on the wet earth as, evading my mother's vigilance, I escaped out of the hot hall into the chill of the night. We called the wild land the hollows. Would he follow? I faltered a few steps along the path, frightened of going in amongst the bushes alone. The dying undergrowth still gave a thick cover. Would he come? Two or three silhouettes appeared at the doorway. My name was called by my mother. I could hear the note of panic. I'm here, I said, out here, getting a breath of air. Your shoes, she said, in a shocked voice, your best suede shoes.

Sometimes when I watch here at the window, a sudden shadow flickers between the tree roots that have been laid bare by successive flooding on the stream banks. A flow of pale grey fur slips down towards the water where amongst the stones it stops for an instant in perfect imitation of a stone. This squirrel is always watchful, full of disguises. Now a rounded stone, now a long slim arm of beech, it moves in startled flashes, freezing at every breath. When it comes close enough, I can see its eyes, as it clings to a swaying branch, its nibbling face, the way a sudden movement of mine stops it dead, like a dead branch swaying with a watchful eye. This guarded nature seemed to lie at the heart of all our dealings. Every move I made was watched with a benign intention. I watched myself. Moreover, the notion of an all-seeing eye was deeply engrained. When I was small my grand-mother had heard me say my prayers each night. God sees all evil and all good. For years and years I had secretly pleaded my case: Father, you are bound to forgive me because I am only a child. But now that I was growing older I could no longer make that excuse. The existence of God was at best questionable. For a long time I had said no prayers. Instead, at night, it was the game that sent me to my sleep. Night after night this ritual let me launch myself upon the sea of darkness. Time and again the eyes resist closing, ache to spring open and see the pencil-line of light that comfortingly etches in the shape of the door, the robe on the door, a hooded shroud, net veils at the window, a stirring of air behind the curtains. I wake from a nightmare in which a man is fumbling to unlock the catch of the window. But the window is always open. Panic-stricken, head under the covers in the thick warmth, I pray: Father, keep us safe this night. I breathe more easily for a while, stifled not by airlessness but by something in the air, listening to the ears throb, lifting, then listening again, more intently, for something else that it might be better to see rather than let it come smothering down. Keep us safe. There is a noise from the open window. Outside in the street people are laughing and talking. Life is going on as usual. It was only a bad dream. Keep us, oh, keep us.

Throw back the heavy blankets and listen. Propped on elbow. The voices make it go away. Is it afraid of the voices? The words of the prayer come back: secure from all our fear. It is only fear then. There is nothing in the night except our own projected images. Now it is possible to cross the stretch of linoleum, to stand by the window, to look down the sleeping street. Two people kiss, pull apart and go their separate ways. One door slams, the other shuts with a dull thump. Now nobody else is awake in the night, for God is only a word. To be good is of no avail. Only if I can stay on my guard will I be safe this night. I watch at the window until my mind goes to sleep, and when I wake it is morning and I am warm in my bed.

On Tuesday evenings my mother helps with the youth club. Only children who attend the church are allowed to join, and somebody has to sit at the door. Several meetings pass during which we eye each other, this boy and I. And at last, one Tuesday night, when my mother is in sole charge, I tell her that I have some homework to do and I leave the church hall on my own.

It is a black, moonless evening. The boy walks behind me along the path. He catches up with me at the gate. There is a short hill. Then he must go one way, I the other. At this point we both stop. We do not talk. We have never exchanged any words at all. Our eyes have done all the work of arranging this meeting. I look my way. His fingers bite into my arm as he pulls me his way. I am incapable of resisting this mute invitation. My legs are weak and I am breathless with excitement. I let myself be led into a back yard at the top of a neighbouring street where, without kissing me or offering any preliminary remarks, he crushes me in a frantic embrace. There is a rough-hewn coping stone on the top of the yard wall. It seems as if he wishes to grind me against this stone. I struggle but he is astonishingly strong. His body begins to jerk convulsively, and it occurs to me that something is happening to him that is out of his control, for at the same time his hold on me weakens and I am able to spring myself from the trap. My heart pounding furiously, I begin to run, but he does not give chase. He shouts something, and to save face I call gaily over my shoulder: Night!

Unlike the spiritual passion that has been snuffed out so easily by the tin can, this physical attraction did not disintegrate at a touch. On the contrary, I felt that I had narrowly escaped not because he was so importunate, but because the temptation to stay had been almost overwhelming. I never looked at him again, nor did he ever make any approach to me. But I sometimes felt that by remaining aloof, by refusing to lose myself, I had lost something else important, a kind of innocence. On one level it was impossible for a good girl even to imagine tolerating such a relationship. I ought to have been offended by his presumption. But at bottom I knew that he had been the innocent. He had read me right. Part of me.

It was as if my body had not just a life but a will of its own. Its actual life carried on from day to day, eating, excreting, moving, resting, and from month to month, bleeding, and from year to year, growing, shedding nails, hair, flecks of skin and even beginning to show lines. But none of these functions was interesting to me in itself. I might feel hunger or a pinching shoe or an itchy spot, but these were nothings compared to the need I had felt that night. It was as if my body had reached out directly for the very thing that would meet this need, regardless of all the paraphernalia of civilisation. Magnetised by this event, my mind kept being drawn back. I could never again pass the street corner without feeling the hard stone biting into my back. What if I had been unresisting? The end house was empty, its yard full of trash and long grass. Suppose I had lowered myself on to the ground behind the wall and breathed: Come. What would have happened next?

A few weeks later this boy joined the army. It was common knowledge with us that the army was a kind of training ground for the most inadequate children. Soldiers came from homes that could not cope, often because of poverty or neglect. When he visited the church on leave that Christmas the uniform and the shaven neck more than ever put him beyond the pale. About this time one of my cousins was also persuaded into the army; he had been a bothersome son to his mother and he had got a girl into trouble. It was as if these two instances represented the bottom line – the worst in social and moral terms that could happen to me. I could become embroiled in some unsuitable association and end up living on a council estate in a world where people communicated in grunts and jerks. To me at this time this threat seemed a not remote possibility, a not entirely unwelcome alternative to the rigours of respectability. To fall over that wall would be to be free for ever. When the boy laughed, I felt an answering laughter, a delight in simply being, an energy that seemed, if only momentarily, to impel me in that other direction.

Mornings I walked to school, muttering, this energy transformed into words. To see was not enough; I had to say what I had seen. First the yard gate, then the street, the shop at the street corner, the row upon row of houses that gave place across the main road and along the avenue to suburban gardens. Then uphill past a paling fence behind which there was an old house. Then tennis courts. A road lined with trees. One two three four five six seven houses. And then at last the school gates. At first it was enough to stride along at a steady pace, but later this was not enough. More slowly I had to walk; more and more slowly to give me time. Going home. First the gates, made of wrought iron, painted black, tipped with gold, spear-shaped and interlinked. Then the laurel bushes. No, again. Try again. Play the game properly and be precise. They are large bushes with big shiny leaves splotched with yellow like leather. Poisonous, my mother says, flattening the specimen between pieces of brown paper. Is this true or false? We can make our own book of leaves, she says, and write labels in our best hand-writing, but the dip pen blobs the ink and we never fill more than two or three pages: elm and alder and elder and ash. There is a waywardness in the mind that runs down alley-ways into dead-ends and loses itself in thickets. But where is the mind when the mind is absent? Is it still there? Does it sleep? Or is it switched off like a light that is disconnected from the current? Back. Back. Pause by the old house and see the stone façade with its eight casement windows, four above and four below, the door red, no, the door maroon, no, no, the door dark red, wine red, dried blood red. Tarragon wine at Christmas, waiting on the tray at midnight after the carol service. Bitter-sweet and aromatic. The plangent music of the organ. The passion of our Lord. The blond cropped head of the boy. The trace of alcohol on his breath. The braying voice out of tune. No, no. It had to be in order. The door. Then on. The road with a steep camber, new-surfaced. Chips of stone. Whitish grey. Like stone. Like crushed ice. Impacted ice. No. Like chipped off stone. Stone. Stone. Stone. Chips of stone. Sharp. Embedded in tar. The tar black in places. Slowly. Go more slowly. Get it right this time. If anybody goes by pretend to duck down and tie a shoe-lace. Stand still and look for a stone in your shoe so that whoever is walking behind will get in front and leave you in peace. Where were we? The road, remember? We were speaking of the wonderful road. A dried runlet of tar on the grating like a runnel of black treacle down the edge of a tin. The smell of treacle toffee burning on the gas ring. Ginny licking her fingers. Then the leaves of the laurel. Big yellow irregular spots on green. A poison tree, says my mother, never ever lick the leaves. And the stone house with the blood-red door. Dark blood red, we agreed. Dark blood-red door in house with eight windows in trim grounds behind new fence where the wood under the peeling bark is smooth and pinkish like skin on the back of the boy's new-naked neck. A poison tree, says my mother, never ever lick the leaves. But the tree of knowledge is an apple tree with round red fruits nestling in its boughs and a snake twining around its trunk.

Everything is always splitting open to reveal these seeds. The need to examine these germs of meaning gives a thrust of urgency to these solitary rambles. In the later years of the war I used sometimes to wander away from the boarding-house amongst the side-shows and awnings of the Golden Mile to spend my pennies in the slot machines or to buy sugared waffles or hot dogs or cough candy or little saucers of shrimps soaked in brine. One day I paid my pennies to go into a booth lined with glass tanks full of fish. A crocodile stood in a few inches of sluggish water. The man who had taken my money lifted out a snake for me to see. The snake was a warm brown, blush-brown, braided like the embroidery skeins in Ginny's box. Here, the man said, feel its skin. The snake slowly stiffened and coiled itself round his wrist in a loop. The man said: Nay, lassie, it's got no venom, this little tiddler. I stroked its neck. It was not a slimy, slippery thing. It felt cool and hard and dry. The man took it from his arm and put it round my neck like a collar. Tail-end and head-end. And marks on the body that were the vestiges of lost legs. Because God punished it and made it to drag along the ground in the dust. Now and then its forked tongue flickered as its head swayed from side to side. I waited politely for the man to finish taking pennies at the door, but I was not frightened of the snake because he had told me it was not dangerous and I believed his word. In the same way I had not been frightened of the boy. Something in me each time knew that these were not the real dangers. Only if I let them be. I was glad that I had held a snake. It made me feel brave. At the corner of the street, had I then been cowardly or had I simply chosen a different way? But however much I might speculate I knew there was no going back.

That Christmas as always the dinner was held at our house because being nearest to the church we could borrow a trestle table and two benches. The aunts brought their crockery and cutlery in baskets and shopping bags. There was a large chicken and a piece of pork, a great tall stem of sprouts, and two kinds of potatoes. Every bowl and dish was needed for an assortment of sauces and stuffings. All morning two steamers hissed with home-made puddings. Sixteen people would sit down to dinner: the aunts and the husbands, my mother and father, the six children. And always the family was joined by a childless couple from up the street, a bachelor friend of one of my uncles, and a big tall woman who had no relations and was a living-in maid at a grand house near my school. When my mother had been a girl in service, this woman had been kind to her, and for the whole of her life until Violet died of cancer, my mother went on paying this debt of gratitude. Once a year in the summer she came for tea, and again at Christmas, carrying her box of sugared almonds. Mostly she sat upright, at attention, smiling. Having no one to talk to at home, she hardly ever used her voice, which was rusty and hesitant, full of curious affectations and absurd mistakes. At the table she would suddenly say: Are you all in good health? Everybody would nod encouragingly at these attempts at table-talk, which had the temporary effect of silencing conversation. Sometimes a tear would appear in the corner of her eye and she would give it a shy dab with the corner of her napkin. And people would say: Nay, it's not right for folks to be on their own at Christmas.

Every year these great occasions took weeks of planning and saving. Each sister owned one large linen table-cloth, Irish linen with a device of shamrock leaves worked into the weft, presents from another sister. Lovingly laundered, these were placed overlapping on the trestle, which, once erected, made it impossible to move about in the room. People squeezed into their places, graciously making light of the inconvenience. My mother and my aunts organised everything. Together with the children they carried down the borrowed furniture, made the lists, hoarded the jars of pickles and the dried fruits. On the actual day they mashed and drained, and beat, and served, calculating to the last fibre of meat and inch of crackling how much was needed for every plate. Yet, strangely, when the guests were all assembled for the great culmination, it seemed as if my father was the presiding spirit. Flushed, excited, voluble, he filled the little space of the kitchen, urging a mouthful here, a sip there, cracking jokes, checking the children, talking politics with the men, shouting No, it will never happen in this country, shouting Gravy, more gravy, shouting Yes, pick up the bones with your fingers, fingers were made before knives and forks, teasing Ask Violet, Violet will tell you all the best people use their fingers. Squeamishly I pick up the wish-bone, and snap it with my sister. The one who gets the biggest fragment gets the wish. Everybody claps. I close my eyes and wish for something to happen. I want. I want. But what is it that I want? My youngest aunt winks. She whispers: I bet I can guess. I feel myself going hot. Her eyes widen. She whispers again: Don't tell anybody his name or it'll never happen.

In the afternoon the children were sent out for a walk, while the men went into the sitting room to play cards and the women cleared up in the kitchen and made sandwiches for tea. Being neither one thing nor the other, I helped to dry the dishes and was then set free. I did not want to walk to the park in a posse of children, but there was no other way of getting out of the house. Where are you going? my mother says. I pretend not to hear and go into the hall to put on my coat. Already it is getting dusk. On each side of the front door there is a narrow stained-glass window: green glass leaves and red glass bells. Air bubbles have formed minute imperfections in these coloured morsels of glass. When I was little I used to delight in seeing the world outside changed, distorted and marvellously suffused with a red or green hue. Now, I have outgrown this pleasure. I open the door. If only snow had come. Every year the crooning voice promises a romantic transformation. If only something would happen. But out of doors the day looked ordinary. It could be any day. The weather was not seasonal; it was humid and grey and heavy. Moisture beaded the pavements. Where are you going? my mother says. But there is nowhere to go. I slam the door. Nowhere, I snap at my mother, there is nowhere to go. Hurt, her best pinafore saturated with soap-suds, she throws me one reproachful glance before returning to her guests. It hurts me to hurt my mother, but I do not know what to do with myself on this Christmas Day. Every room is full of people. We do not use the bedrooms except at night, but I run upstairs to look at my presents: new vests, handkerchiefs, a leather shoulder bag like the ones the teachers have at school, a book.

I sit on the stairs and dip into the book: *The Mill on the Floss*. The title is oddly appealing, though at first its meaning eludes me. Floss is something I have seen long ago in a spinning mill where my Lancashire aunt was working: all along the shed there were great bundles of silk stuff bursting out of bonds like the filaments of seeds erupting out of closed dandelion clocks. That was floss. I have learned to read very rapidly, skimming along the lines and just picking up enough of the sense to satisfy my hunger to know what happens next, so that the description that explains that Floss is the name of a river does not engage my attention. There is a girl in the story. The girl has aunts and a brother. The girl reads a book – *Pilgrim's Progress* – that I have not only read, but actually own, a book that lives in the kitchen cupboard along with the knitting patterns and the box of recipes. The girl has a doll that she loves and hates with a passion that I understand, for I remember piercing the stomach of my own rag doll and the sick shock of finding it full of straw. Suddenly I realise that I am not in the realm of fiction at all. This is a kind of reality. Always, in the reading, books take on a vivid life of their own, but the discovery of an actual connection with the world as I know it and live it myself is staggering. Always, reading has been a pleasure and a treat, but in one great leap reading has become a realisation. Somebody, another person, has been there before where I am now. The book becomes a kind of proof, a vindication, a testament to my own reality.

A day or two later I finished the book. My identification with the girl – Maggie – was so intense that I experienced her destruction as a total catastrophe. After the short Christmas break my parents returned to work and I was left alone at home to look after my sister. Henceforth, day after day, my sister would play freely in the street. I stayed in bed reading because it was the warmest place. The incomprehension of the family, the cruelty of the brother, the torment of her unfulfilled desire, the injustice of her death, the absolute and wanton waste of her life seemed unbearable. I rose from my bed, weak at the knees, drained. In the kitchen I found the porridge pan waiting to be cleaned, considerately filled with water by my mother to make the task easier. I put my hands into the sludgy mess. This was the first on my list of jobs, a small, easy thing by comparison with what the girl had suffered in the story. Confined within the house, I railed against a fate that could be so restrictive. It never struck me that things might have been told a different way. Indeed, it seemed impossible that her life might have taken another course. Given the conditions, the rules of the game, there could be no other outcome, for once the girl had erred, even in thought, she was doomed to suffer. And in thinking at all – or so it seemed – she had been guilty, while her stupid brother, being incapable of thought, was allowed a moral victory. So it was and so it must be for ever and ever amen. I never doubted the authority of the writer: there was a force in those pages that was taken from the rhythm of nature – from the river and the trees and the red, wounded earth. And thus, in one great leap, my own intermittent pessimism was given a licence to become absolute.

Seven

Tonight the moon rides high, ringed with opalescence, gliding through clouds that glimmer with a faint, silvery radiance. I am still haunted by recollection. Often, then, I lay on my bed in a kind of stupor, while the husks of my outgrown days fell away, leaving me vulnerable and exposed, but not altogether without recourse. Because at that time, I began to compose my thoughts on paper, inventing my very own self; and while my isolation seemed most complete, this second self became a constant companion. I had outlived the den in the hedge. The girl who had been my friend left school to go to work. For a little while I too tried to leave. One Saturday I stood outside the town library trying to force myself to go inside and find out whether it was possible to work there, because I thought I might feel at home amongst books, but I did not know how to ask. Another day I stared in at the newspaper office, stiffening my resolve to go inside and ask for employment, but, again, I was too nervous. From the moment that I realised I was now of an age to support myself, I became convinced of my own incapacity. Terrified, I was relieved in the autumn to be received back into the hum-drum of school, where everything was familiar, where I had to contend only with my own lack of initiative. I became one of that tiny few, a privileged nucleus of girls who went on studying, a decision made not by me or by teachers, who could not have thought much of my ability, for I was no better than the many who left, but by default on my part, and because I was deferent to my father's wishes, since he placed a value on education.

In the summer that I was sixteen, after the public examinations, those of us who were staying on had no time-table. The rule required us to stay within the gates, but we were otherwise free – to read or swim or play tennis, or simply to stroll about the grounds. From time to time a teacher would call on us to help with a stock room or cupboard, and this created a feeling of being behind the scenes, of being well-established in the school. A little room with a kettle was provided for our use. At first I was shy of these girls. On wet days I went into the library. On the first sunny day, I sat outside with a book for company. One girl who had never played games, because she was asthmatic, had permission to use the piano in the music room when it was free. It was pleasant to hear first scales, then snatches of melody come bubbling out of the open window. After a while another girl came to sit on the wooden steps by the tennis court. I looked up absently so that if she ignored me I could pretend to be deep in thought, but she smiled a smile that was very wide and at the same time sleepy. It was a good, strong face, not pretty, for it was narrow across the forehead and broad across the jaw, a foreign face, that was beautiful in its own fashion. I knew the girl was a Slav, because she had been in my form for five years, but she was not one of the poor refugees from my district; her parents were on Christian-name terms with some of the teachers. Her name was March. A strange name. Suddenly I found myself saying aloud: My birthday is in March. She was writing something in an exercise book. Mine too, she said with another slow, very humorous smile. After a while she tossed her book gently into my lap, saying: Please read and tell me what you think. Out of the scribblings and crossings out and reworkings, eventually I made out: When the wind stirs in the castle moat wild rose petals fall and float. Puzzled, I said: Work? Now? She laughed. It's a poem, she said. What for? I asked. Again the smile, but even before she explained that she was doing it for herself, out of interest and pleasure, I had already realised my mistake. I looked down at my book in embarrassment, fearing that she must think me doltish, but when it was time to go and put the kettle on for break, and the pianist leaned out of the window and waved, she said to me in a friendly voice: Coming? I remember being transported with joy at being asked to join this girl.

These two girls became my new friends. In the previous year my old friendship had begun to wear thin. The habit of communing aloud in the den had come to an end. With these new friends the talk was never to be so intimate or so spontaneous. But it was more informative. Their lives were more integrated than mine – at least on the surface. March lived in a house full of books. To write poetry was an ordinary thing for her to do, just as she was a linguist because her parents spoke several languages; and indeed many of her poems were translations. At first I wanted to be just like these girls. And thus to begin with I began to write because writing was one of the things they did – like reading or music. But very quickly this writing, which I called poetry, became habitual with me, and then compulsive, because once I got started I simply could not stop.

Poetry – reading and learning and later explicating the lines of verse – had been an enjoyable feature of school life since infant days, in part because, unlike quadratic equations or contour maps, it involved no mental strain. All gone, my grandmother sang, scraping the custard from off the bottom of the dish where the cow leapt over the moon and the dish ran away with the spoon. Sleep tight, she sang, as she chomped up the spice with her sharp yellow teeth. Sugar and spice and all things nice. In the very beginning poetry seemed to grow out of language in the same way that grass grew between the cobble-stones in the street, growing there in spite of the sprinkled poison because it was in the nature of things to grow green in spring-time. But it was not invented, it was simply there.

One day late in the war the limping man-teacher who was a wounded airman was standing at the blackboard pointing to some words. Read that, he said to me, read the lines aloud. I stared at his chalk-writing; it was slanted and trembly, difficult to read, with capital letters at the beginning of lines instead of after the full-stops. It was the first poem I had ever seen in writing. His forehead was lightly furrowed with horizontal lines and his eyes seemed to dance. Take a breath at each punctuation mark, he said, not at the end of a line. I began to read: Crouched in his kennel like a log with paws of silver sleeps the dog. His eyes were dancing. At first I could feel my heart beating very fast. Very good, he said, when I finished, you are a good little reader. I long for an excuse to go and be near him at his desk. A silver dog. A little silver man and a little silver woman, he in a top hat, she in a poke bonnet. If only he would come to where I am sitting and put his hand on my shoulder and give me a friendly pat. The words of the poem are almost meaningless. What is a silver dog? Does it mean an ornament on the mantelshelf? Or perhaps a lucky charm? Or is it something out of make-believe? But though I am left in some confusion about the meaning of the poem, I feel no doubt at all about my reading or my feelings. If only he would kiss me there on my cheeks or on my nose. And because poetry teases the mind and pleases the senses all through my school days, it remains one of those lessons on the time-table at the thought of which I feel cheerful.

In the early days of the grammar school, formal composition had been given every week. Sometimes we read a ballad or a sonnet and for homework would be asked to write an imitation using the same metrical form. These experiments had been easy and interesting in a technical sense, but the content was insignificant. The most enjoyable part was receiving a good mark. There were enviable girls in my class who were clever at everything. I imagined that such cleverness gave them a wonderful immunity from suffering. But for me it was not enough to receive full marks for a poem. If there was a speck of red ink – one red comma or dot – my father would frown when he opened my book. Again and again before trusting my work to the neat book I wrote out my exercises in rough, and each time I made modifications, always trying for perfection. Finally, my mother used to ask me to read these poems aloud to neighbours and friends, so often that I knew the lines by heart.

But the writing I now began to do for myself was not mechanical. The lines came with great rapidity, sometimes in rhythmic or rhyming patterns that were recognisable; sometimes the lines refused to fall into preordained shapes and yet, to my inward ear, the music they made seemed authentic. This writing was not like work, but nor did I think of it as play. It was not a game. It was a telling. It was also a keeping. In this respect it superseded the game of naming that belonged to the night. Unlike the game, which was fluid, it left evidence, a residue. It gave me a kind of stability. Instead of being always at the mercy of time, in which the torrent of impressions was forever swept away, I could hold back the flood for a little while. It was like taking part in a rescue operation, dredging up the drowning items out of the day's dreaming, restoring equilibrium where all was flux and change and terror and death. All at once the different mental activities, dispersed and desultory as they had always been, converged in this one activity. In writing, thinking and feeling came together. Weak and vague as I felt in every respect that seemed important, in writing I felt confident and energetic, as if I was in direct contact with a mysterious source of power, a power that was neither personal nor supernatural, though it contained elements of fervour and elation.

Now I was often glad of my own company. I used to walk home by the most sequestered paths, so that I could think in peace. It was as if I had come through an archway out of some dim corridor and found myself overlooking a misty panorama, of which now and then I gained glimpses of something complete, matter-of-fact, vast and intricate, maybe, but open to reason, accessible to meaning, ultimately negotiable. Such visions had the effect of irradiating even the most commonplace experiences. That walk home yielded such impressions that I sometimes had to run in order to catch them before they fled into obscurity. The words came in great spates, formless, line after line, disconnected images, exclamations, exhortations, line after line, on the bus, in a corner of the library, in the cloakroom hidden behind coats, in lessons, in my own room, in the kitchen on the fender by the fire, hugging myself in a knot to keep warm, scrawling with a too-hard pencil on cheap mottled paper in a school exercise book; until, drained, distracted, overwrought with excitement, I came back to find the scene mysteriously altered, sapped of its colour, imbued with the desolate aftermath, the nullity.

The moon. Maybe it was simply the phases of the moon that dictated these swings of mood from elation to despair. A few years later I read in a text book that young girls are prone to fits of exaltation. But at that time there was no mention of the menstrual cycle. Except for my mother's initial shy attempt at explanation there was complete silence on that subject. Amongst the girls I knew the taboo was absolute. I myself adopted a lofty indifference to this monthly emission which my mother called the visitor. My female relatives discussed female complaints, but there was a quality in their kitchen conversations that discouraged confidence. A kind of prurience, a mixture of the covert and the prying, the inevitable concomitant of a secrecy forced on them by convention, was abhorrent to my mind. Thus, nobody ever suggested that there might be anything chemical in the giddy alterations of prospect that afflicted these dawning years. Impossible now to know whether, in any case, greater knowledge would have been serviceable. To what end? Except that even with the benefit of a rudimentary scientific education, even having dissected the reproductive organs of a rabbit, there was something in the nature of the taboo that prevented growth, so that for all the intellectual questioning, the probing into metaphysics, the juggling with ideas, the heroic vision of myself I clung to as I revolved obsessively around myself, the centre of my universe, there remained an area of vulnerability, a closed part, a place that was primitive, infantile, regressive, requiring solace and support.

In school my subjects were literature, religious knowledge and ancient Greek, the latter purely by chance because I was good at languages, there were too many girls that wished to study German, and when the teacher had suggested an alternative I had not dared to demur. As for religion, that was my choice. From the very beginning, even though logic had made me doubt the literal truth of the scriptures, I had enjoyed the lessons. For a long time I had been content to go to church, to attend at the rituals, more out of habit, out of respect for my mother's wishes, out of enjoyment of that society and that special atmosphere of heightened emotion that emanated from religious occasions, than out of actual belief. My new friends called this lip-service hypocrisy. I chose to study religious knowledge as one of my examination subjects because I told myself I needed a more secure basis for rejection of something I instinctively mistrusted – mistrusted even when it was reconstituted in the guise of other beliefs, in the form of deism or pantheism, for example, by those romantic poets with whom it was suggested, mistakenly, I should find myself in sympathy. It was not so. I infinitely preferred the writers I studied in Greek. Both the harsh, passionate outpourings of the plays and the dry, systematic dialogues of Plato appealed to me far more than the grandiloquence of the romantic poets whose raptures seemed alien: they spoke another language than mine. In literary essays I learned to make a superficial adjustment of my mind, adopting certain received forms in order to be able to make appropriate gestures of acquiescence; but in the lessons on Plato I was given techniques of analysis that helped me to think. To examine ideas was to unravel the mysterious intricacies of the mind. This process of introspection which seemed to integrate thought and feeling was justified socratically as self-knowledge. All of a sudden, instead of seeming to be merely a series of disconnected parts, knowledge appeared to me as a seamless whole, into which my own mind was woven.

My Greek teacher had no other student. We were put in a kind of closet off a laboratory overlooking a playground marked out for netball, bounded by a high stone wall behind which ran an avenue of chestnut trees. The teacher was young and black-haired. To me she seemed pitifully ugly at first. She had coarse skin with open pores in her nose and home-knitted woollens that exuded a faint odour of stale sweat. Her lips were big and soft and rather shapeless, and she wore badly applied lipstick and silver bangles. She was fresh from university and unused to teaching. She had no method. Half a dozen sentences we would translate and then we would stray off into interpretation. Is the tree really there? she asked. Below, in the yard, there were girls playing a game of tig, before the teacher stilled them with a single blast of her whistle. Then there was vocal silence, except for the occasional sharp calls, exhalations of breath. We could hear the heavy ball thudding and the short shrills of the whistle. The line of trees was touched with autumn, the huge umbrellas of the leaves stained by the dying sun, which cast long slanting shadows across the ground where the feet beat in excited scuddings. Is the tree really there? Which tree? I remember a kind of mental daze; the tangled arms of the trees, blurred, red, shedding leaves into the thin wind, a sudden triumphant shout from a girl in the yard, the faint yet rank odour of the woman's secretions, the chill air of the closet with its bottles of crystals, its tiny corpses in preserving fluid. Is the tree there? She was teasing, loving the game. She wrote down a title: 'The Theory of Ideas'. In a flash it seemed to me that there could be no proof. The tree – like God, like fear and all its phantoms – might be merely an aspect of the mind. Yet at the same time, for my purposes, the tree was there. It was essential to get hold of it before it lapsed away. I was under an admonition not to let it go. At break I stared at the wall with its pattern of moss and lichen, its tiny nodules of bright orange mould; and at the fallen leaves mashed by feet, knowing myself that I too would fall and be joined in all that falls, bemused, driven by expectation, aware at last of the fatal incompetence of the word.

Never mind the moon. It was a phase is all I am saying. I came to read lyrical poetry at last not for its meanings but for its sonorities, its raptures. In the school library I read every book of poetry. In the town library I was allowed two tickets for fiction, six for non-fiction. Each week I took out eight books and forced myself to read the six factual works for the reward of two novels. I did not understand Kant, Hegel, Schopenhauer, but I wanted to become a learned person; and through these books I discovered my own simplicity. I acquired a small notebook in which I wrote down the names of each writer I had not read, and when I had made his acquaintance I gave him a red tick: Apollinaire, Verlaine, Gide, Tolstoy, Turgenev. Certain books made immediate sense, but others taxed without yielding any profit. The ambition that drove me was not social – I scarcely shared these reading expeditions because I met nobody that was interested – but I was seeking a companionship of the mind. And the ones that made most sense, from George Eliot onwards, were mostly nihilistic, even when, like her, they affected a melioristic position. This was not something I understood then in those terms. I simply took from such writers feelings that sounded a note of recognition. In the death or submission of these heroes and heroines I saw foretold an inescapable doom. A sense of hopelessness, of impotence, of profound dejection, confirmed in these pages, was thus given authority.

Home. School. Home. School. The old familiar routines continued, but the end was in sight. It was difficult to conceive an existence outside these institutions. And from this time – the time when I would soon be released – I was able to perceive incompatibilities between the two realms, incompatibilities that had much to do with language and with class. For after the age of sixteen, the group was composed entirely of those girls drawn – like the teachers – from the middle classes, who lived mostly in semi-detached houses, whose parents did work that was non-manual and somewhat better paid than the labour of my relatives.

When my mother came to school on special occasions she was shy of this world and wore her very best clothes and manner. She was afraid of being considered a lesser person. The other mothers had the assurance born of having been properly dressed and shod all their lives – or so we assumed. Much, much later I may have deduced a more complex set of reasons, but at that age the economic basis for our differences was the one that seemed pre-eminent; and ultimately I come back to this cause, as the one that is amenable to alteration. The rest is mystification; it exists, but, being diffuse, is not open to immediate change, whereas these material variations could be stopped. All the same, my mother's timidity – half-apologetic, half-resentful – was one of the scars of class that set her apart from me. Because once I was given the entrée into this other class – into homes where there were books, pictures, chintz coverings on good old chairs – the distinctions between people that seemed so important to my mother began to seem insignificant. I began to resent her self-effacement. I saw those other mothers, substantial, easy in their ways and their purses, supported by husbands who earned enough for all their needs, who owned a bank account and knew how to write a cheque, saw those women as being coarse-grained next to my own mother, saw them as slack-minded, dull, spoiled. At times I burned with a sense of injustice: I could not believe my own relations, who were less well-off than these people, were any less deserving or less human. On the contrary, my nihilism of that time was aggravated by an awareness of human waste. My sense of urgency, my need to find reciprocity and to express myself, were heightened by the bitter knowledge that within the lower classes there was a potential energy that would never be released, and which could – if only it were ever harnessed – become the motive power for great change. But this would never be allowed to happen by these others. On the contrary, I knew that in each generation a few of us had been singled out by pure chance for special treatment by a system of selection that was actually no system, that was only a pretence of justice; and I knew that those that had been excluded were in essence exactly the same as myself and these others. Yet, whatever my private affiliations, I had been admitted to the middle ranks. I no longer belonged in the street. I felt myself to be a member of nothing.

In this way, believing that I now belonged to neither world, I made a virtue of necessity. Literature became my province. Existing amongst books and the names of books encouraged a retreat from actuality. In both of the real worlds I was weak; but in the imaginary realm I was a remarkable person with a host of alliances. I had only to pick up a book from a shelf to gain access to this other place, to be transported out of myself, to gaze into a magic mirror, in which lay reflected the real appearance of things, ordered, composed. And the existence of these authors, who offered me this sanctuary, was the one great guarantee that ultimately it might still be possible to achieve that intimate union with another human being, the promise of which seemed to lie at the heart of all our language.

I longed for the coming of this other self, the mirror-image, the kindred spirit – not as a figment, but as a real person. It was for this reason – because I had to be ready, to be recognised – that I became obsessed with my own appearance. I spent hours in my mother's bedroom, looking at myself in the long arcades of glass. I washed my hair every day. At every turn I examined my face, now in glimpses trying to surprise myself and thus discover my true, my objective identity, now in long silent trances when the features seemed to dissolve eerily into a faceless blur, leaving a sense of partial annihilation. But only partial. Because always, as if through a chink in a wall, another self watched these watchful selves in a process endlessly thrown back upon itself like those cloudy greenish images down the long mirrored corridors in my mother's room, where, opening and shutting drawers, inhaling the wafts of naphthalene and lavender, poking amongst their private possessions, collar studs and cuff-links, a striped tie coiled in the semblance of a tweeded snake, a single leather glove with a frayed fingertip and a button like an amber bead, I sometimes came upon secrets, secrets that could produce a pang of guilt and that urged me to ask no questions. Thus, once, rummaging, I had come across, hidden amongst my mother's camisoles and handkerchiefs, a length of rubber tubing, bright brick red, that ended in bulb-like swelling, an object curious and sinister, which somehow obscurely I knew not to mention. It was as if recognitions of this kind were always preceded by a knowledge that was amorphous, diffuse, a set of disparate hints and impressions, inferences drawn almost by accident from half-heard conversations, from incidents barely registered except at the periphery of the mind. And the effect of this piece-meal acquisition of such knowledge was to create gaps and misconceptions, false trails that led inevitably to wrong conclusions.

Something never told. Blackpool. There was no prospect of the war ending. A faint echo of that time – martial music, a news-reel voice with a curious tone that was both important and jolly, a noise like walls falling with the sound of distant thunder. A blackness criss-crossed by pencil-lines of light. Then flames, fountains, fumes of vapour. Mesmerised, I watched the war, watched the shaft of light that cut through the darkness, shooting out from the little window in the black wall behind us high above our heads. Shadows. The scene on the screen was black and white. A white, snowy field on which black shapes lay sprawling. Puzzled, wanting to find out how the shimmering beam made those pictures, I wriggled round till I was kneeling on my tilting seat, which creaked on its loose ratchets. Someone said angrily: Keep still. Two girls in the street had asked permission to take me to the cinema in the afternoon. Giggling on the way there, they called it the bug-pit. It was a wet day. I wanted to stay with my grandmother. Let Grandma have a rest, said the lady of the house. Anxiously, I clung to her dress, the dress that was the colour of port wine with a design on it in white, ellipses that looked like spinning sixpences. Never mind Grandma, said the man. Here. A whole shilling. Enough for in and for sweets, my grandmother comforted, leading me by the hand to the front door, where the two big girls were instructed each to take a hand. Entranced, I watched as the crinkled curtain crept slowly upwards in silvered ruchings, while the writing on the wall wavered and blurred and finally leapt into true focus, the half-licked barley sugar in my fingers unheeded beside this mysterious transformation.

The girls were on my left. Next to me there was a vacant place, then the aisle. The seats were plush, prickly at first on bare legs. Now and then somebody shone a torch along the rows. People passed each other, stood up, lit cigarettes, coughed, hushed, softly spoke, but by and by these minutiae lapsed into complete absorption, so that his arrival went unnoticed. I never saw his face. Perhaps I had fallen asleep – certainly the picture was over my head, and I could make no sense of the narrative, so that only fragments impinged in the nightmares that put the cinema out of bounds: a man in an iron mask, a bed with silken covers round which the soldiers wait for a prince to wake, their spears pointed at his neck, an enamel plate like the one we used for apple pies on which the doomed prisoner writes his message. I came back into myself with a jolt to find that something knobbly and hard had interposed itself between my bottom and the seat of the chair. Involuntarily I squirmed to get free of the object, and then realised that whatever it was had got inside my knickers and that somehow I could not budge. All of a sudden I understand that there was a man and that he had got hold of me with his hand, his nearest hand, in such a way that I could not get free except by crying out for help. But it was a silent place. Once or twice when children around us had been rowdy the usherette had come, saying: Hush, hush. The man was hurting, but the shame and the alarm were much worse than the hurt. A long time passed while I waited for it to go away of its own accord, a time that ends in the blackness of lost memory. Eventually, the film ended and they must have taken me back to the house. The following summer I started school, and it was the same girls that took me across the road to the big iron gates. I remember one of them looked Chinese because she had black hair across her forehead in a straight fringe. Her name was Betty. Doubtless the man disappeared into the streets, carrying with him the knowledge of this furtive violation, which remained secret with me, as much because it was unmentionable as because it was deeply shocking.

114

Which means that even then there must have been prior knowledge. Nothing connects with nothing. I knew it was wrong. I knew I had been victimised. I knew that I was defenceless. Henceforward, I knew that it was necessary to be very careful. Beforehand, I clung to my grandmother. Afterwards, I knew I had to arm myself. In an oyster an irritant may produce a pearl. In me this trace of evil operated like an inoculation. I became guarded. The slightest premonition of danger set up the alarm. I was always on the watch for an enemy, who, almost at once, ceased to be specific. My mind – so far as its surface was concerned – rapidly became a blank. Nevertheless, when, coming out of the school gates, finding myself alone, the girls gone, I had to find my own way back – across the main road, along a ginnel, behind the gas works, down the alley-way into the dead-end street with the pink and white and blue houses – I was quite simply galvanised by terror, running so fast that I felt my heart must burst out of my throat.

Or, calling at a house to play, sent to knock at a door in the street there at the seaside, or later at home sent on an errand to a shop where a man might be serving at evening-time, coming out from behind the counter and flipping the sign on the door from open to closed, his buff overall flapping, brown buttons hooked through darned eyelet holes, a whiff of sawdust and bacon ends and oranges in blue tissue paper, it was as if antennae picked up these signals, as if my eyes hastily sized up the distance to the door, the click of the ready lock, as if my senses could measure the gap between the permitted transaction – the proffered list with its ticked items, the silver counted out from the soiled palm – and that hidden violence from which not even a child could be exempt.

Unless perhaps fear is born at birth in the violence of that rupturing? Water and light and breath and flesh – water fire air earth – all coming together in one great gasp of terror that becomes, almost instantly, within seconds, minutes, hours, a greedy grasping, a reaching? When do my sister's eyes begin to see? When does she begin to know that she knows? At two three four five six seven as she grows I wonder what she knows. We are within reach of each other – divided by only ten years – but this decade is sufficient to prevent us from sharing our childhood. Sometimes when she is sleeping – for now we lie side by side in the same room – she mutters in her dreams. I press my hot face to her face. The hair is damp on her forehead. I open the window to let in the air and turn back one of the blankets. I want her to love me, but when she is awake I am frequently bored and impatient in her company. Every holiday, every evening, I am supposed to look after her, but mostly I am relieved when she wants to play out of doors. On wet days she is a nuisance. We have no story books at home that I can read to her and she never brings books home from school. At each stage of her early years I can remember quite clearly being her age, but just as I was locked inside myself when I was little so she is inarticulate. Sometimes I ache with love for my sister, but there is no way of expressing this love – no way of pleasing her, of keeping her happy – except by letting her go.

My mother does not understand this principle. Home. School. Home. School. My mother wants to keep me within the narrow compass of this familiar pattern. I need change. I need to get out of the house. I make excuses to take messages to my aunts in the evening simply to get out of doors. Because all the time I am wanting to find the person. Tea-parties and shopping outings with my school-friends are acceptable safe excursions, but my friendship with March languished after her father kissed me in the car when he was giving me a lift home. I wanted so much to arrive at our back door in a private car, but, understandably avoiding the cobbles, he chose to go the front way which had a wider, asphalted road. Nobody ever sat in the front rooms in those days of coal fires, and the street was dark, the windows unlit. The car was a black box with red leather upholstery – like a taxi. I knew it would be childish to ask him to wait while I knocked on our door, so that at least my mother could see. I pulled ineffectually at the handle and he leaned over to help me and planted a kiss firmly on my mouth before letting me go. Pleased and abashed, I tumbled out of the car. I had wanted him to kiss me, teased him to kiss me, but afterwards I never wanted to see him again. He had taken an unfair advantage.

Every day, from that time forward, brought with it the prospect of such conquests. Home. School. Home. School. The same even tenor of existence – except that in addition to the inner life that had always flowed secretly below the surface, there were now these actual encounters, these often fleeting contacts that were promoted by this need of mine to form a connection, a need that could be stimulated by a glance, a voice, a face only half glimpsed in passing; this need which grew in a moment like some rampant weed that covers a desert after sudden rainfall and which, exposed to the light of day, as suddenly expired. This was a pattern: sudden passions that ended in sudden desolation. So that once, pierced to the heart by the slant of a cheekbone, I followed a man up an escalator in a department store, up three flights, pausing while he wandered from counter to counter, fingering the goods, then down again, three flights, desperately willing him to submit to my will, buffeting through crowds on the mezzanine, keeping his coat within arm's reach; until, turning, his gaze falling full upon my face, realising or not, he makes his way towards me; whereupon, appalled, terrified, I shake off the compulsion and force myself out into the town. Only to realise – though the particular confrontation has been avoided – the craving is still there, the dreadful need, the craziness that makes me feel I am a huge vacuum expanding, expanding, and that in order to save myself from annihilation I must suck everything else inside myself: or simply consent to disappear. I gulp air. I close my eyes. But nothing changes. When I open my eyes I am on a tram and the conductor, caressingly, is taking the coins from my palm. I am upstairs on the back seat. I smile. The tram-car is empty. He sits down next to me and puts his hand on my knees. Suppressing a yelp of alarm, I jump to attention and hurtle down the steps. I walk, exhausting myself, demented, thwarted. It is evening. Yellow light and rainfall glint on the tram-lines: the two parallel lines curving into the distance are two knives turning in my heart.

At night, I write in my exercise book. I feel very strong. Then, in those moments of recollection, it all makes sense. It is all of one piece. The exercise book with its crumpled blue covers slides down the hillock of my knees on to the counterpane which my grandmother made out of strips of figured cotton, inside of which there is an old grey army blanket instead of wadding. All gone. Allgone, she sings, crunching the last bit of butterscotch, which she slips from her mouth into my mouth so that her syrupy spit trickles down my chin. All gone. No amount of sentiment can ever reconstitute these images in their true form: they are gone. Even the moon has changed its nature, attached new meanings with new technologies. My Greek teacher teases out interpretations. Was Socrates' wife a shrew? she asks, smiling. The idea of philosophers having families suddenly telescopes time, so that when in the spring the sixth form visits Italy I will stroke the pleated garments of stone people and stare into their lidless eyes, remembering the white cold angels in the graveyard, my grandmother, my dead girl cousin with her red hair. A dreadful cognisance of mutability that links us with the ages past. All gone. I kneel on the cool pillow and, with my elbows on the window-sill, crane a look down the lamp-lit street. If I open the casement and lean right out, the city will unfold like magic, its roof-tops faint and slatey in the moonlight, its houses in packed phalanxes marching across the lost hills. By day – chimneys and smoke-stacks, millyards and back streets – it seems a far cry from what she, redolent of her own class, calls the cradle of our civilisation; but at night, almost within ear-shot, I hearken to the voices that, preserved only by chance in scrolls, in curious volumes, echo down the long ages, beckoning me to make my own record. It is needful. For without history there can be no progress, only lost people, caught in the treadmill of circumstance, like those voiceless slaves, and those wives, whom she – her earnest eyes intent upon imaginary trees – mentions in passing with a rueful shrug: the flaw in the Greek perfection.

My style was elevated, orotund, much influenced by the Bible and by these classical studies and by reading Victorian literature; and when I became vocal in class this fustian quality was evident in my speech. At home I was fluent in a familiar idiom. Falling between two languages, I made idiotic mistakes. But if my mispronunciations and periphrastic locutions were sometimes comic, if the press of thought led me to be absurdly high-flown, this also worked in my favour, winning for me a reputation for originality that helped to give me confidence. After years of feeling only my ineptitude, of feeling only half alive, I felt suddenly larger than life. I became alert to fine shades of meaning in texts that had seemed initially to be inert matter. Above all, the production of such texts was immensely reassuring, because it seemed to imply the existence of a real world into which I would in due course be admitted and where I would feel at home. For at hand, in the immediate, apart from my family, there were only girls, who, on becoming friends and engaging in mental and social intercourse, would eventually flag or become distracted and thus fall short of real intimacy.

I was always trying to force the issue. I seemed to be constantly straining for something more strenuous, more exacting, more enthralling than was ever available. The girls I now knew – in some respects far cleverer, more competent than I, more effective in leadership and in the strategies of work and games – seemed nevertheless oddly weak-minded. The softness of their upbringing had left them disarmingly soft and simple. Some of them had baths every day, and the bloom of babyhood was still on their skins. They had made friends readily enough, but what was in them did not go far: there was no resistance, no rigour. Yet there was some comfort in such contacts; and sometimes, reading, sharing a line or two of poetry, a kind of peace ensued, which was simply the feeling of being accepted within this circle, provided that one behaved with a certain decorum, showed common sense, was studious, not loud, courteous to others, mindful of the teachers, displayed conduct ruled by maxims that my own mother certainly thought not amiss. These girls were essentially conventional, disapproving of those attributes that my mother would have called commonness, and which meant not only all signs of an overt sexuality – red fingernails, bleached hair, pointed breasts – but also any kind of coarse vitality. And she was happy when I brought these girls home to tea, because she thought I had found my own level and was bound for the good life, whereas in reality – except for these brief spells of well-being – I suffered almost constantly from a sense of estrangement, which was terrifying in its intensity; so that struggling to be like these others, copying their clothes, their gestures, their speech mannerisms, I was privately censorious and critical of their ways. Racked by a constant consciousness, aware that I was always aware, eaten by an insatiable hunger, I simply drifted along on a current of opportunism, doing whatever they did, going wherever they would go.

Thus, when the Italian trip was first projected I was eager to go and my parents readily agreed. But it cost a great deal of money, more than a whole month's wages, a sum larger than my mother ever had in her possession at one time, since they were paid by the week and lived from hand to mouth. My mother promised to put a few pounds by each week, but this proved too difficult, and as time passed and I became panic-stricken at the thought of reaching the day of payment and having to withdraw from the arrangements, I imagined the disapprobation of the teachers who had stressed that the agreement was binding. I imagined them making an announcement in the hall when the party was assembled: One girl has let us down. I imagined the humiliation of being singled out and the impossibility of explanation. Money was always a problem, because even with two wages there was never enough to meet our needs, since my mother, who administered our finances, was never able to budget for that impulsive spending which was one of the compensatory pleasures of what my father called wage-slaving, a way of life that encouraged a kind of minimal hedonism. Apart from the necessities of life – the rent, rates, heating, lighting, clothes, food – which her theoretical book-keeping could cover in theory, the money dribbled away in dozens of small disbursements, so that by the end of each week we were waiting for the wage packets, out of which my father extracted a small sum for his gambling. And when he had a bad stretch of losing, mid-week, he would come back for more, pleading with her in the hall to let him have enough for the tram fare and the first race, their voices lowered to keep me from knowing, because any reference to racing was surreptitious, lest I should be tainted by his vice. My mother always came back into the kitchen from these encounters, flushed, tearful, but relieved that she had let him go, because his presence, especially when he was surly with frustration, cast a gloom over our evenings, making the temptation to give in to his demands greater than the desire to remain solvent. Later, I understood that the actual amounts were very small, representing a symbolic squandering rather than a serious outflow of funds, which were quite simply too small to allow for the material expression of all their needs.

My mother was not satisfied simply to survive. Her conception of the good life required the keeping up of appearances, improvements to the house, new net curtains, a dozen antirrhinums for the strip of garden, a washing machine with automatic rubber rollers, items which mortgaged the wages in advance and caused aching hours calculating on the backs of spent envelopes in secret, because such large purchases were frowned upon by my father, whose only rashness was in regard to the small sums staked each day, which, like secret sips of alcohol, satisfied his compulsion. And because I could see the sense in her acquisitions, whereas his passion remained obscure, I entered into her affairs, which involved endless schemings, the drawing up of lists and room plans, so that in the evenings while I worked at the kitchen table, and she knitted, darned, ironed, baked at the same table, we constantly adverted to these common concerns, which took us on forays to the town centre at weekends on excursions of spending from which we returned with our funds dwindled to the limits of real danger.

When I realised that the Italian trip threatened my reputation, I told my mother that the teachers required payment week by week along with the dinner money. In this way I managed to extract a few pounds regularly, which I secreted in an Oxo tin at the bottom of my wardrobe. The dread of her finding this hoard was not as great as the horror of being found wanting at school. I knew she would be hurt and shocked by this subterfuge, but I also knew that if a big bill were to arrive in the interim and she were to know of my funds, she would be sure to inveigle me into surrendering what I had saved. And so I hardened my heart. For years, when the rate demand came and the money was not available, she used to send me with small amounts to pay off the arrears, and thus keep at bay the summons that she feared. I would stand in the queues at the rates offices with the other defaulters, poor people, averting their eyes from each other, ashamed of their poverty and their incompetence, shuffling patiently in the crowded office, while my mother waited a few blocks away, not wanting to be seen driven to such straits. So that if pride forced me to be hard on her in this matter of the school trip, it was because I had already learned from her the importance of such appearances: impossible to reveal to teachers that we could not make ends meet and to let those girls know what it cost us to meet on their level.

In the photograph taken at the station on the day of departure, I am pictured at the end of a row wearing a coat – a good coat of Donegal tweed with a red silk lining – which was borrowed for the holiday from my youngest aunt. All the girls are carrying real leather shoulder bags; all are smiling. Nothing much distinguishes me from the others, who may, for all I know, have gone through similar shifts to arrive at the same point of departure. To me the distance seemed immeasurable. Which is probably why, in the Roman forum, in the Coliseum, in the streets of Pompeii, I brooded rapturously on those idyllic presences, the dead, whose remnants invested those alien landscapes with a mysterious affinity. At dawn I stole out into the hotel garden where white gravel crunched underfoot and white urns spouted a foam of purple flowers; and watched these forms unfold out of the darkness until the pale pearl, the milky radiance, cleared and left me marvelling at the astonishing clarity of a smokeless sky. Whom could I tell? Who would listen? How could I get it all together into one whole? Where was the beginning and the end? I picked up white chippings, splinters of marble that glittered in the azure light. I put a velvet flower in my mouth. A waiter in a starched white coat clapped open a shutter. His sleepy eyes sought mine. I smiled invitingly, wanting to open my arms to the world and say: Come. Seeking consummation, I felt in my bag for a pencil and wrote on my pad: Here begynneth the day. Tears tickled my cheeks, dried on my cheeks, as the crown of my head began to throb with the heat of the sun.

121

Eight

If it were that simple. This expression, cast up like driftwood on the shores of my repose, lies there for a long time. A fragment. A broken exclamation that belongs to a tangled mass of thought and feeling. Thought and feeling. The presence of the second self provides a constant commentator. I call this other self my consciousness, yet I retain an idea that the first self, the one that has always lived inside my head, is the real self. They are not, however, in opposition. It is simply that the new self is always educating the old quiescent self. A friendly Socratic dialogue is taking place in which the two selves examine aspects of experience that were formerly inchoate, interfused: thought and feeling. Are these labels useful, necessary or true? The process of differentiation sets up vibrations of alarm, because my old self's sense of reality is in jeopardy. Everything is questionable. This scepticism can be exciting in company, but in solitude, pushed to the limits of enquiry, the mind reveals itself as a composite thing, not a coherent entity. Surely, in some sense, the old familiar self was also aware of its own existence? How would it have been possible to summon up memories without a separate will? And when the mind goes blank, is that a switching off or a waking sleep? And where is the self when, fastening upon a tree, a cloud, a leaf, a bird, there is suddenly only a tree, a cloud, a leaf, a bird? It seems there are rifts in consciousness – clefts, fissures, splits in the self that sometimes produce a sense of sick foreboding. At other times the discovery of being a not-person is curiously exciting. Is it the self that pours the glass of milk in the morning? Is it the same self that walks back along the same road at the end of the day? Where has the person gone that crushed the spider on the stair? That sat at stool in the dank lavatory under the area steps, eyes riveted on the spider to keep it at bay? Inside, in the cavern of the skull, is there anybody there? Is now the real thing? Or now? Or now? The moments drop away like the notes of a melody falling into silence. I keep trying to retrieve the droplets in order to achieve some kind of stability; to be able to say: it was then, then, I was my real self.

It is December. Thirty years ago. At school a Christmas party has been promised to which the boys of the neighbouring sixth form have been invited. I am to have a new dress. On Saturday my father takes my sister to a football match so that my mother and I can shop in peace for material, early, because my aunt will need time to make the dress. All afternoon we search without making a choice and on the way home I am close to tears of disappointment. My mother, entering into my mood, says comfortingly: It would be lovely to be rich. Her face is grey with exhaustion. I notice that her bloom is fading. She is still a pretty woman, but there are lines that run from her temples into her hair-line, from the edges of her nose to the corners of her mouth. She is a secret smoker, for my father does not approve of smoking, and so we ride upstairs on the bus, where the windows are fogged and the atmosphere is rank with the fumes of smoke, stale breath, damp overcoats. She breathes deeply, inhaling with relief and holding the cigarette low between draughts in the hope that nobody will notice. I too disapprove of smoking, but I am more irked by this pantomime of lady-like behaviour. I evade her sympathy, hardening my heart against her, feeling that to draw close, to share in her sentiments, will somehow weaken my own position. I cannot share either my discomforture or my fixed will. Both seem inadmissible. Indeed, my entire life begins to seem subterranean, covert; and this sense of being enclosed, cut off, shut in, unable to assert myself, gives me the feeling that I am looking at everything through a darkening glass. It affects everything; even the light has a certain quality, offering a bleak, cruel illumination. Thus her face is grey, but so are all the other faces. Mostly they are poor people, hurrying home to enjoy the best evening of the week. Saturday evening. Bow-legged old women and stunted old men and jaded women and pale youths with slick hair and girls with red-gash mouths heave themselves on and off the bus at the stops, jauntily hitching up their bursting shopping bags and thrusting their way into their own streets. And though I try to burrow inwards in order to avoid connections, I feel a powerful affinity with these people. When our eyes meet, there is instant understanding: we are all in the same boat.

At the bottom of my mother's shopping bag, from which exudes a strong reek of leeks and celery, there is a poetry book, picked up from a stall for sixpence: it is called *The Ship of Death*. The thought of this acquisition cheers me. Later, I will read, and the long effusion will leave me troubled – and convinced: wanting to be active, free, happy, it will be years before I recognise that the poem is only a celebration of melancholy, not a guarantee of disaster.

The bus jolts from stop to stop. I make a patch in the steamy grime so that I can gaze down into shop windows, lifted out of gloom, in spite of my ill-humour, by the thought of the book, and by the splashing of coloured light on to wet black pavements that snatch a mirrored radiance as the bus lumbers past. Already the shop windows are beginning to be decked for Christmas with imitation icicles, tinsel, synthetic snow. The streets are emptying and grids are springing shut across entrances. The bus is packed. It halts in front of a department store where, in one display, a window dresser is working with huge bolts of shot silk, which she tosses nonchalantly over the nude dummies. My longing to acquire a dress made of one of those shimmering fabrics is suddenly acute, extreme, urgent, and as the bus pulls away, the combinations reel in my mind: violet with blue, red with amber, silver grey with green. Which is it to be? What is the cost? Am I as slim as those models, strange sexless shapes, the colour of calamine lotion with jointed limbs and featureless faces and hair like spun glass?

At night, in secret, I look at myself in the mirror, but only at my face, my neck, my shoulders, my arms. I am whitish fawn, and in the cold of the room the undersides of my arms are mottled with a pattern of blue veins, while the hands dangle clumsily, knuckly and red. I try to sleep with them tied to the headboard to make them slenderly pale, but common sense prevails when they begin to throb. In any case, I am in the middle of a book which compels my attention, a book by Virginia Woolf called *Mrs Dalloway*, which is like a net full of wriggling silver-fish, all slippery meanings and strange, half-submerged intentions. I need my hands to turn the pages. I do not understand the book in my head, but I am spellbound, engrossed: I feel I understand. Once again, here is a book that is telling me there is no hope. It will be half a life-time before I am able to put this feeling into any kind of perspective. When I finish reading I surface and find the world is grey, inscrutable, menacing. I do not know how to grasp hold of this unkind

124

reality, with its intimidating paradoxes, both impervious and yet intrusive, complex and yet oddly banal. The beaker of cocoa on the stool next to the bed looks at me with a blunt, uncompromising stare; it is maroon, with a thick, imperfect glaze, flawed in the firing, so that the rim is speckled and rough. I know nothing of these pottery processes. I do not know how anything came to be as it is; and this incomprehension invests each item with a forbidding power. Moreover, I cannot even explain this complication of feelings, so that when the teacher asks – as she is bound to do – whether I have enjoyed the book, which she has recommended to me, as I perceive as a mark of her especial esteem, I can only nod mutely, ashamed of my own incompetence. Whenever I am put to the test, my heart throbs so painfully that I can hardly say a word. If she asks me precise questions, then I will be able to single out suitable answers, but our discourse will fall short of actual communication, for something has made me reactive, limited. How would I ever dare to tell her that when I finish reading I am in unutterable despair? That I stuff the sheet into my mouth to stop the screams from ripping out of my throat and waking the house? Or that I am rescued from this anguish by the thought of a green dress with the sheen on it like grass in the park in the early morning, when the whole family – mother, father, sister, aunts, uncles, cousins – go on a picnic to spend all of a summer Sunday watching cricket; and, before the morning dew has dried, our footprints, pushchairs, trailed shopping bags make bright green tracks across an expanse of pearly grey. And everybody is squabbling about deck-chairs and blankets on the grass and about whether the damp strikes through and who has forgotten the red flask, and I am thinking, as I fall asleep: How much will it cost, how much, how much, how much will it cost, the green dress?

But to what end a green dress? It is one of those hundreds of attempts to create the perfect image, the female complement to that ideal figure, the promise of which seemed to lie not only in the literature, in the philosophy, in the religion, in the common culture, but in the very language, and thus in the actual texture of my own being. There were no pictures in my house, because my father did not approve of scarring the walls with picture hooks, but in Ginny's attic there were two prints, taken, I think, from some magazine and framed with passe-partout under glass. Twinned images of a boy and a girl, each robed in white and blue, haloed in daisies, seraphic, they floated in flowerly meadows, their shining eyes sharing a smile of vague beatitude. I used to lie in bed, willing myself to enter their blissful twinship long before I had learned to read. Even the flowing calligraphy of the captions seemed magical; and when I could read, when I knew that under one the title simply read *Little Bo-peep* and under the other *Little Boy Blue*, it made no difference. Their spell was already cast.

At the same time, running counter to this drift, another tendency linked this promised land with regions of terror. Only a few months before my cousin had died, there was a scene at my house when she was fetched in from the air-raid shelter, where she had been caught doing something with a boy that was forbidden; and was beaten by my aunt, beaten until my grandmother and my mother both dragged my aunt, weeping and screaming, on to the sofa, behind which I was cowering. I cannot see my cousin, only my placid aunt, her face contorted and swollen, falling upon the floor, where she grazes her forehead against the fender and is revived with smelling salts. But when, that spring, Ginny died, I asked myself whether God had taken her as a punishment for that sin which had taken place in the shelter, which I was forbidden to enter, and which – for a short while after the war – stayed in our street, dark and dank with the stink of cats and dogs and maybe tramps, my mother said, or rats that lived in the sewers and might come out at night to roam the gutters of the town. And then, too, that other morning, when sleeping in her attic under the twin, the charming pictures, I crept out of bed to relieve myself in the chamber pot that was at her side, and found rosy swirls of blood clouding her water, her blood that came out of her body, which might have been – it seemed later – an omen, a warning of that untimely death.

So that deeply, deeply, rooted together, twisted together, these intimations – desire and fear, love and death – fed my imagination. Thus I went to a party in a green dress sewed by dead Ginny's sad mother. My youngest aunt gave me six rhine-stones which my mother sewed on to a strip of black velvet ribbon to make a choker, and my father had a win at the dogs and bought me a pair of black velvet slippers. The family conspired together to create me, just as, when there was a death, they fished in cupboards to find a black hat, a pair of gloves; or at holiday times, they clubbed together to go into lodgings at the seaside; or later still, when I went to university, they gave me a pair of sheets, two teaspoons, an old trunk that had belonged to my grandmother, and that had been stored all those years in an attic, its strip of oil-cloth desiccated with age. Their sense of kinship meant that they saw it as their duty to me – as with all the children of the family – to push me upwards and to keep me within bonds. To be a good girl was the essential thing.

I went to my party, dressed and armoured, desiring and yet dreading the very encounter for which such social operations were a formal preparation. But such a formulation gives no force at all to the fervid state in which I approached such gatherings, then and for a long time afterwards. Every going out was a potential culmination. Every return was a descent into despair. At every moment to ask: Is now the moment? To look and ask: Is he the one? Suppose I say simply I was searching for the right man. And that this was now a compulsion far more pernicious than any addiction, because the addict is perceived by himself and others to be deviating from a norm of health, whereas this obsession was the supposed norm: this was permitted – within the limits of the law and custom – was encouraged by every expectation, was seen as inevitable, according to a pattern that reached back to the origins of life itself. My mother pinched my cheeks to make them look rosy; and then – surreptitiously – touched my cheekbones with rouge from a little worn box. Be good, she hinted, tucking one of her lace-edged handkerchiefs into my evening bag, watching me down the street with a wistful gaze. Because the mere existence of language itself seemed to imply the necessity of a fellow communicant, just as the anatomy of the flesh, while never openly investigated, nevertheless seemed to be fashioned for its mate.

Locutions and circumlocutions. Clumsy. Clumsy. But there is nothing simpler. The simple statements leave too much out of the reckoning. A girl looking for a boy. An intolerable reduction. First, I did not see myself as a girl in the least. Girl. Boy. Man. Woman. I denied utterly these distinctions. I envisioned myself as a person. Daily, except for my own father, I mixed only with people of my own sex. Daily, in my reading, I was in the company of writers – men, women, Lawrence, Joyce, Woolf, Eliot – in whose ideas I experienced no sense of ill-fitting. If there was a human entity at all, I myself was that entity. My conscious self never conceived the possibility of myself as defective by nature as a woman. On the contrary, when – at that first party – some humorous remarks were passed about the inferiority of the female, which was the first time I remember hearing such an idea articulated, I was merely amused, picking up the notion and tossing it back as if it were merely an insignificant token in the game of flirtation that would, when the games ended and serious intercourse began, be put away in a drawer along with the draughts and dominoes and other childish toys.

The party was held in a classroom that had been cleared of desks and decorated with paper chains and Chinese lanterns. One teacher worked the record-player, while another ladled out a fruit drink from a big kitchen bowl into paper cups. We stood along one side of the space in our party frocks, while opposite, the invited guests, stiff in their tweed sports jackets or best blazers, pretended to talk to each other in a manly indifference, until their own teachers prodded them into asking us to dance. It was like those church socials, except that instead of a mixture of generations, we were all of an age. To be chosen was the essential thing, for to be left standing when the music started would be to lose face. The fact that as girls we could not do the choosing was simply accepted as one detail in a ritual; it was not examined or challenged at all. To my relief, I recognized one of my own cousins. In a large family like ours, such relations might be mere acquaintances; his mother was my father's sister, but we met perhaps only once or twice a year. Nevertheless, in relief, we greeted each other like old friends. He was a bridge for me, as I was for him, in this uneasy meeting-ground. We danced together, and when the tune ended we stood together, familiar and yet oddly almost strangers, trying to think of things to say. He was a good-looking boy, moderately tall, fresh-faced and almost totally inarticulate. What are you going to do next year? I asked. At the far end of the room the woman teacher started another record. I want some red roses for a blue lady, wailed the singer. I'm off to work in a bank, my cousin blurted, as he steered me inexpertly over the lumpy floor. This is an excuse-me waltz, the baggy-jacketed master shouted in a desperately jocular voice. To my delight, a fair-haired youth, who – it was rumoured – had a scholarship to Oxford, and was brilliant, disreputable and iconoclastic, clapped a hand on my shoulder and stammered at my cousin: Sorry, but it seems one must play these absurd games.

For a moment or two we laboriously circled the floor. Then a curious conversation ensued. The content was simply an exchange of information. The boy, however, played the part of a person constrained against his will to participate in an undignified ceremony. His

128

performance was comically self-deprecating. He had no aptitude for dancing and was encumbered by self-consciousness: As you see, he remarked, dancing is not my forte, but it seems one must be a good sport. Following his lead, I fell into an affectation of being romantically inscrutable in order to conceal my perplexity. I was not at all sure how to behave towards this incipient genius, and so I made soulful eyes and gave a distant smile. Every now and then he tripped over my feet. I had always been fond of dancing. My father had taught me long ago at family weddings and church socials. I had never enjoyed running or playing sports, had never willingly engaged in any physical exertion, but dancing was of the spirit. It had always seemed to lift me out of myself. It was a potent excitement. It made me feel strong, elated, reckless. I want some red roses for a blue lady, the singer repeated again and again. Round and round we twirled. After two or three revolutions another boy cut in and then another. I was asked to dance again and again. And gradually the one lit corner in the dark school building, the shuffling school-boys, the notice-board disguised by crêpe paper – all dissolved in the heady atmosphere that was created partly by the music and partly by my being chosen. I felt witty, confident, charming, and this success was important to me, because it gave me the status of an attractive person within the group of girls. The crowning triumph was to be asked to be walked home by the extraordinarily bashful blond youth, with whom I immediately fell passionately in love. But of course my father came to fetch me. We walked home in a bewitched silence through frosty streets.

If one must participate in these absurd games, he had remarked. It was a game of course. But I was good at the game. And it was not just a game after all. It was a need, in the first instance simply to talk, but which, constantly lifting me off balance, produced again and again that sense of disequilibrium which is popularly called falling in love, a sense of letting go, of losing control, of being animated by subliminal forces that promise a more direct and more total release than mere verbiage. Of course, the injunction to be a good girl meant that this inclination had to be fought with reason. The game was the result of this tension between desire and discretion: desire was inadmissible and so everybody played safe, teased, chaffed, sparred, fumbled, retreated, took stock, weighed the odds, compared notes, gathered forces, played again. In this way the energy became dispersed. And when, from time to time, a serious commitment was exacted by one of these casual partners, a deadly hiatus ensued. To be asked to be walked home was desirable, but what, given the prohibitions, could one actually do, or say, even, to the other person? Two or three times, having reached this point in a succession of such parties and meetings, I simply switched off, falling out of love within a few days, vaguely alarmed by these vicissitudes, adopting a noble solitude; and then, involuntarily, still driven by the craving to find that other person, I started to search again. The effect of being frustrated in this way was never to diminish the hunger or to cast doubt on the outcome, but to make it more acute, more all-consuming, so that in the absence of real experience, the playing of the game became a constant necessity.

From this time I had my ready excuse to escape from the house. I claimed that at the library I needed to use the big Greek lexicons that were chained to one of the desks. In reality I seldom had recourse to these great volumes, though the idea of this dependency appealed very much to my vanity of being a scholar. I loved the library – its vast, vaulted porch, absurd relic of Victorian pride, its dark, panelled walls, its banisters mounted with the heads of hunting dogs, between the fangs of which, from time to time, to my indignation, smokers would stub out their cigarettes. The reference library was on the top floor of the building, a long gallery, with a row of little gable windows providing recesses, in each of which was fitted a table with a mirror-like surface, and tall-backed chairs, and which overlooked the packed roofs and smoke-stacks of the city. There, with my books outspread, now day-dreaming, now taking stock of the other occupants, now translating one of those sections that my Greek teacher called gobbets, my restless imagination was satisfied by the nearness of other people. At home I pined, fearing that life was getting away from me. Mostly, in the library, there were men: students, elderly men, now and then a rabbi, once a venerable Indian, sometimes school-boys, one or two of whom I now knew by sight. At the best of times my concentration for other kinds of work was weak, but I could usually sink myself in a book. At the library, however, my attention was constantly straying, as I stole a look round the room, or made an excuse to consult the catalogues in order to stroll past the other tables. To ask myself: Is he here, the one? And as I became a familiar of the place, now and then somebody would nod to me. Or one of the boys that I knew slightly would fall into step beside me as I left and we would engage briefly in the game of flirtation, at which I rapidly acquired a kind of facility, and which thus provided the illusion that I was rather powerful; so that from this time, from having been timid and gauche, I began to see myself in a new light and to conduct myself accordingly as a rather self-possessed person. In reality, I was possessed only by one idea: the One. Is he here now? Here? Now?

It was like living at the centre of a vortex into which everything else was constantly being pulled; dangerous, yes, but so exciting that each moment seemed the last. And each moment as it was lived and then consigned yearningly to the past, each moment achieved a marvellous resonance, a clarity, a pungency that set the teeth on edge. I would sit in the library, staring, astounded. All the faces. My eyes sped from cheek to cheek like butterflies on the wing, ephemeral creatures that, dying in a day, are driven to seek a desperate fulfilment of their destiny. I wanted so much to touch the faces. My fingers itched at the tips to trace the line of a crease, softly to stroke the lobe of an ear, to tweak a hooked nose, to take hold of the thin brown wrist of an Arab student, to stare full and long and greedily into the blue pleated irises of eyes and to discover my own diminutive image lying on these convexities. But even to exchange brief glances could lead into perilous and forbidden territory. Many years later an Indian girl told me she was raised in the belief that a good girl must always keep her eyes lowered; and though at first hearing this sounds preposterous to Western ears, it is after all only an advance on that practice of swiftly withdrawing from eye to eye contact with strangers, that avoidance of the bold stare, that assumed modesty which my mother advocated as the proper demeanour for a young girl. Thus, I kept stealing glances, trying to take in what I could, prevented from giving out and wanting to take in more, always more, more. And then I would write blindly, closing my mind and opening the valves of my heart, so that what was left on the page was an effusion which, as I read more of other real writers, as I became more skilled in the art of reading, struck me as more and more inefficacious. What was I trying to achieve in these lines, except release? Of what use where these emissions? True, they gained me a little credit, a little reputation for originality. I read my poems aloud to my mother and she urged me to send them to the newspaper, but I had sense enough to know that there was no market for them there. They were printed sometimes in the school magazine, where they looked convincingly professional on glossy paper, and gained me a school prize. But they achieved nothing else. They were only words on a page. They could never earn me a living. And yet there was nothing else I wanted to do. Where then was I going? To what end this craving to express myself which nothing could satisfy except this constant scribbling? True, at times reading could bring a temporary assuagement of this terrible hunger. But between times, increasingly, I was obsessed by this question: what was I going to do? And always, when I listened for the answer, there was the vortex, the rushing of sensations into and upon one another, the wild beatings and dreadful murmurings of impossible wings.

One evening in the early summer, I came out of the library and found the street suffused with the rose-hued glow of late sunset. The days were lengthening and the air was balmy. Because of the post-war austerity we were allowed to wear ordinary clothes in the summer instead of our winter uniforms, for to purchase two sets of uniform would have been too hard for many families. The new look was well-established by that date; it was supposed to be very feminine with voluminous skirts and nipped in waists and pointed breasts. My circular skirt was made of a gingham woven by one of the aunts that lived in Lancashire. She had the oversight of four looms and used to send us seconds from the mill: calico for sheets, poplin for shirts and blouses, gingham for dresses and table-cloths. I was always well-dressed. I had a bangle on my wrist made out of green metal, and a green jumper. A girl at school had accused me of trying to look glamorous. It was perfectly true. I was obsessed by my own looks. I paid attention to every detail. Everybody – it seemed – approved of this concern. My aunt had made me an underslip of lawn with three tiers of frills on which we had embroidered no fewer than fifty sprigs of flowers, ironed on from transfers. And as we stitched and they talked I sniffed as I heard my aunt saying: I tell you, an education is a waste of time for a girl. Nonsense, my mother said, an education is never a waste of time. Even if she gets married she'll have it behind her if she ever gets left, and there's no telling. Such conversations bumbled on hour after hour. I knew all the terms of reference. Knew, for example that 'left' was a delicate allusion to widowhood, since in the most gross instances of disaster – and never in our family – would a marriage end in separation, while divorce – except for the rich – was almost unheard of amongst our class. When we were alone, my mother and I, and she was grumbling about my father, I used to say: Why don't you leave him then? But it was an academic question. In the end, or so it seemed to me, my father and my mother were like an animal with two heads worrying at a mutual irritant; they irked but never really fought each other. I had always taken her part, because she chafed at his authority, which did not seem to decline as I grew older. On the contrary, he seemed ever more vigilant, checking work he could not understand, watching the hours and the company I kept with a suspicion that constantly inflamed my sense of injury.

If I had not gone to the library, those evenings, I would have been allowed to go nowhere. There was nowhere suitable. I had to be home within half an hour of the library closing. And sometimes on the nights when he did not go to the dogs, either because he had no money or because there was no meeting, he might even ride down to town on the tram to escort me home – not purely because he wanted me to be chaperoned and to check up on my behaviour in public, but partly because his cooped days left him restless: he needed the exercise, the change of scene. Perhaps he wanted to be with me, to be close to me. But of course we never talked on these journeys. To be deprived of gambling made him preoccupied and irritable. And I was vexed at being fetched. Moreover, we had simply no common ground. Just as there was nowhere, really, that they could reasonably let me go for outings. A girl of my age would normally have been working, probably courting. I was still a dependant. The courting couple would go for walks, drinks, to dance-halls, cinemas, none of which was at all a suitable activity for me as a serious-minded – and single – girl. His ambition for me left me stranded in a social vacuum. I would never have dared to do any of those things; or, if invited, have been allowed to accept the invitation. The fear I had felt of him as a small girl stayed with me, lived within me, destroying any spontaneous relations we might have achieved, making me into a mute, resentful beneficiary of his attention. Just as school had for a long time rendered me speechless because it spoke a different language, a difference determined by class largely, a drawback which disappeared only when I learnt the correct forms and the received pronunciation, so he caused me to be silent by the force of his personality. He imposed himself on me. More accurately, he actually deprived me of the power of thought, since the cut-off point came at a deeper level than that of mere conversation. I simply sat next to him in a state of blankness, doltishly, in the same way that children in school faced with a difficult text that they are being forced to study will lose the ability to understand even the simplest elements and will thus appear stupid or will claim that they are bored.

Yet if there was no common ground, neither was there any apparent reason for our estrangement, since I was never disobedient – or not to my knowledge. We simply existed side by side in a state of opposition. Often, if I made a mistake, a trivial error, say, in reckoning the bus-fare, his contempt for my lack of mathematical aptitude seemed to rise in him like bile, so that I sat there feeling withered, almost defiled. It was the same story when he came into the kitchen shouting: Slippers! Such demands seemed to fly into his throat like inarticulate cries of rage, released in a moment of frustration and anger that left me quailing and wounded in my pride. I was so proud of my innocence, high-minded to a degree that now seems fantastical. I constantly set myself ideals of conduct that I had copied from the ambiguous pages of the novels which I now read with a constant hunger. To stray meant to be destroyed. To survive one must become an ascetic philosopher, a woeful stoic, grubbing around for a living like the people all around me who endured years – a life-time – of enslavement in order to preserve the character of respectability. Hardy's Tess, scrabbling in the turnip fields, was the very image of this ideal. Even, once, dismayed by own lightness, I cut off my own eyebrows to make myself ugly, weeping at the sight of my clown face and sneaking into the chemist's afterwards to buy an eyebrow pencil with which to repair the damage. His mistrust seemed to imply a fatal conviction of my inherent weakness: if I could not be trusted to get myself home on the bus, what could I ever do?

The library was in the main thoroughfare of the city, squeezed in between the town hall and the art gallery, fronted by an esplanade with a war-memorial around which low-clipped box hedges formed a shallow bay in which there was a semi-circle of park benches. Two or three tired poppy wreaths lay upon the steps. I sat there, waiting for the bus, a book open on my lap. My father was not coming. The town was quiet, the evening traffic breathing softly, a few tardy pigeons scavenging the spattered pavement. I fixed my eyes on a bird, learning it by heart: the red circlet of its eye, its iridescent breast, the lavender plumage of its wings. Across the road was a group of youths that I knew from the Christmas party, including the one that had wanted to walk me home. We had been exchanging distant greetings ever since. Wanting to be noticed, I slowly walked to the bus-stop. He waved. The others, teasing him, engaged in horse-play for my benefit, until, blushing deeply, he crossed over and told me they had just started attending some art classes. Come next week, he said, dashing back across the road as his bus came. They were all going in the opposite direction, to the better districts of the town. Elated, I abandoned the bus-stop and walked home. I needed space, time, to be alone. I wanted to think out my campaign. I was already planning what I would wear, what I would say at school, what explanation I would offer at home. But I needed no excuse for this venture, knowing that my parents would offer no resistance to an educational outing; and that providing my activities looked like self-improvement every effort would be made to dress me in the most fetching style.

The following week I went to the art lecture, bolstered by one or two other girls from my class. The subject was surrealism, a strange new concept. We looked at slides of feathered women, at blue horses prancing by pink rivers bordered by avenues of purple trees, and at a man, himself a figure of romance, who muttered terminology into a black beard and who, by introducing the notion of the interior landscape, released into meaning some of those earlier moments of stress and dislocation, so that afterwards the sight of my mug of cocoa, its congealed skin draped in minute folds on the splayed, clumsy lip, was both more and less threatening: less because it belonged to a whole category of things seen in a perspective that could be shifting, directional, blurred, disorientated by mood; less because it was thus explicable, had precedents in an esoteric but none the less identifiable culture; and more because it confirmed the primacy of mind over matter, indicating the danger of subjectivity, opening up the possibility of slipping over one day into complete nightmare, from which there might be no egress. And this experience had about it a grave excitement, a sense of importance and contemplative delight, against which the immediate thrills of pursuit and conquest – the blond boy sitting a few rows away, the possibility of being walked home surreptitiously through the dusky streets, the prestige of being a sought person – resonated with that special note of dreadful meaning that I associate with certain earlier moments, moments that remain discrete in the blur of memory: the disembodied hand in the cinema, the blue-beaded embroidery in the attic, the white hunched shoulders at the kitchen table shaken by sobs, the slimy factory yard that began the descent into pandemonium.

Already how I regretted the loss of innocence. How ashamed I was of my own affectations. I had no spontaneous being. A shadow had fallen between myself and my other selves. And it was for this reason that the ironic fiction of our time, the lucid, jaded prose of Joyce, the lyrical acidity of Chekhov, had such potency, became authoritative, seemed to sanction, even while they derided, those acute sensibilities, simply by confirming their existence. For I was never merely the feathered girl in the painting or on the pebbled shore, but always also the eye of the painter, the cry of the poet. The inherent danger in this split, the potential destruction at any time of the one by the other, was not evident to me then, so that divided, impotent, blinded and silenced as a totality, I oscillated between different modes, and was thus inconstant, conforming outwardly to that infamous fickleness that was supposedly the prerogative of woman.

A few days after that lecture I decorated my bedroom walls with a pattern of postcards, which I stuck on with drawing pins. It was Saturday. The fair-haired boy had invited me to go to the theatre, and my mother, timidly, hesitantly, agreed to let me go, though hinting that we should perhaps keep it a secret. In the afternoon there was a roar of rage from my father as he flung my card on to the kitchen table. They were all reproductions of famous paintings, madonnas and still lifes, interiors and landscapes, inoffensive in themselves, meaningless to my father, for whom they merely represented an injury to his walls. His anger was terrifying. The cards, crumpled and desecrated, lay scattered over my homework. To protest was unthinkable. Even to pick them up and look at them to check the damage would have been construed at that moment as an act of insolent rebellion. I bowed my head and submitted; fearing that my projected evening was also about to be spoilt, I calculated, as the storm raged, whether my mother would have the courage to let me go out once he had left the house, or whether she would use this incident as an excuse to keep me home.

For if I feared my father, if I had always dreaded his intervention, at least, in the past, I had been able to count on her support. But from this time, when I began to form alliances of my own, she also conducted a campaign of coercion, using not threats, but appeals. Often, helping me to prepare my clothes or letting me share her lipstick, she looked upon me with a sad face, as if I was a lost soul. Sometimes, as I bent to put on my shoes, she too knelt, as if in supplication. And always, as she stood on the step to wave me off, tears would spring to her eyes, tears that told me she was lonely and that begged me to be a good girl. Or she would even run after me, as if driven by a compulsion to take hold of me for one last time, to kiss my cheek, and arrange a strand of my hair. It was as if she who as a young mother had been so remote and had left me for weeks at a time in my grandmother's keeping, now seemed to long for closeness, pretending to offer me a clean handkerchief on which she spilt one or two drops of her precious perfume. And then, bravely, almost as a joke: Be good now and don't be late.

For half a year I had played at being in love. But studied now at close quarters the face was wrong for the part of a lover, more cherub than angel, with a tendency to bashfulness and a slight oddity in his physical coordination that may have been simply youth. But he was supposed to be clever. His scholarship to one of the Oxford colleges had earned him great prestige and he sported cravats and cryptic remarks that seemed to be daring at that time. He was thought of as a rebel, since he had refused to join the cadet corps and would not play rugby, idiosyncrasies that his teachers tolerated only because he had brought academic distinction to the school. Instead of being grateful towards his teachers, he was patronising, almost lordly in his attitudes. I was in awe of him more for his received accent than for his quick tongue; he lived in the part of town where there were gardens and tree-lined streets, a fact that I made much of to my mother, since this meant he was an acceptable escort for her daughter. My mother was fond of the idea of eligibility, which seemed to meld together notions of elegance and respectability. In the gossip with my aunts, when any girl was being courted, they were always keen to establish the basic facts. Was he a single man? Was he a good wage-earner? Was he a good-looking, clean-living fellow? Then my mother would ask with a giggle: Is he an eligible bachelor? She had always been a great reader, and in the best stories the lucky heroine could be raised in station. No sensible woman ever went down a step. I played on this idea in order to get my own way, for to be going to the theatre – rather than a cinema or dance-hall – was posh. Wistfully she waved as I teetered in my high-heeled shoes down the lumpy, cobbled street, crying at the last moment: Remember, don't let me down!

At the bus-station we met shyly, and, clumsily taking my elbow, he directed me along the road, not to one of the big theatres, where we would have been treated to a dose of high culture, but along a dingy

137

alley-way to the variety hall. Surprised, I settled myself happily enough, too taken up by novelty, as well as too unsure, to ask questions. I was no stranger to variety shows, because they were one of my father's great treats; he always bought large boxes of chocolates and at matinées ordered tea on a tray in the interval. But then, to my chagrin, I discovered that in this play the regular turns were punctuated by strip tableaux, in which naked ladies, singly, in pairs or in groups, lay in frozen attitudes – as slaves or harem girls or kidnapped virgins – while some loin-clad giant, whip at the ready, presided in silent menace; and an amplified, disembodied voice recited some pitiful doggerel verses that explained the scene. Afraid to catch the eye of my companion, I sat bolt-upright, determined not to reveal my mortification, but showing it in spite of myself, because conversation was now impossible. Next to me, he sat in an abashed silence in a theatre that was half-empty and in which – apart from me and the strip-tease artistes – there was not one single woman.

On stage everything was bathed in a reddish orange light with a great many draperies of nylon net. There were snakes and animal skins, and even animal howlings and the sounds of lashing, but everything was completely static, because the law did not allow any movement. This fact, I think, he did whisper in my ear, just as, I believe, I managed to mutter loftily: How boring. In actuality, though these were the first naked bodies I had ever seen, and though the context was supposedly erotic, it seemed merely bizarre, asexual and tawdry. We were close enough to see the laxity of tired muscles, the inelasticity of ageing skin: the chained maidens were not maidenly. They were simply undignified and improper. What is more, the element of sadism did not impinge because there was no conscious connection in my head between sex and violence, so that the sniggering Cinderella, the simpering goose-girl, really did appear like something taken arbitrarily out of fairy-tales as in a church pantomime, and simply vulgarised. At the same time I felt the boy had perpetuated an offence against my modesty. I experienced the violence only as a personal affront. I knew it was wrong to bring me into such a place. It was an act of deliberate humiliation. I should not be able to tell my mother or any of my friends where I had been taken, nor would I be able to regard my escort – ever again – as a proper person. This judgement put him beyond the pale of serious consideration, and so settled the debate I had been having with myself: he was not the one. I felt relieved, detached. And I watched peacefully, registering each image critically, preoccupied more by this process than by speculations about my companion.

Later, over coffee, he admitted that he had done it for a dare. He praised my coolness. He never alluded to the show. We talked politics. We walked home instead of taking the bus, and going through a little park, he tried to catch hold of me and give me a kiss, which I managed to evade. He was surprised and disgruntled. And that was my only revenge. He took me to the corner of my own street, where, nervous of being caught by my father, I noted that he too was nervous, but for a different reason. He peered uncertainly into the back alley-way, as if he felt threatened by the strangeness of this territory. Seeing it through his eyes, I knew it seemed not just a poor district, but a place of alien people. There was something almost doll-like in his fair face that was so different from those of working people. That was my parents' expression, to indicate people of our kind. I do not think I had ever heard the term working-class. I had no jargon with which to define these differences, yet the impressions were quite precise, for the boy seemed soft and very clean; he looked as if he had been bathed every day with warm water and fine soap and dried on big fluffy towels. Besides, his speech was very fluent and elaborate. It did not belong to the streets. He had no struggle with meaning and was consequently relaxed and yet oddly insensible. He called me a parvenu. It was a new word. I knew it meant he saw me as an anomaly. And I was flattered by this distinction. He kept on trying to catch hold of me and nuzzle me like a young donkey. And I kept fending him off. When he drew his face towards mine, pouting his pink lips for a kiss, I wanted to laugh. He seemed like a toy that I had long outgrown, one of those rag dolls with a porcelain face, that over the years of use lost both the firmness of limb and the power to captivate. He was only a straw man with a limp-rag body. But when, at the corner of the street, having been permitted a peck on the cheek, he ran off, jog-trotting into the night, to become, in the fullness of time, a tax inspector, a headmaster, a chief of the water board, a captain of industry, or simply a manager of Marks and Spencer, I remained behind with that abrupt sense of panic, of leakage, as if my contents, my stuff, was too thin and vaporous for containment.

I walked up the street towards the house past the yards, the faint reek of dustbins, the glimmer of televisions behind curtained windows, crying. My father was in bed. My mother was waiting to hear about the play. I told her a story, not wanting her to grieve. She was rolling her fading hair on to metal curling pins, her face strained, a pile of ironing on the kitchen table. I picked up one of my school books, pretending to read. Don't read too late, she pleaded, don't let your Daddy start shouting. She threw the dregs of the tea-pot on the fire-back to damp the ambers, which hissed softly as the wet leaves began to singe. I heard her mount the stairs, undressing on the landing in the dark, then his voice. Is she back? Yes, soothingly, she's back; she's a good girl. Tell her to put the kettle on and make us a cup of tea. Irked by his dominion, I ran the hot water to speed the boiling. Other tap, he shouted. Meekly, I carried the tea upstairs, and stood beside the bed while he finished drinking, and then I went down again and sat by the dying fire, afraid to add a lump or two of coal in case he came and caught me, thinking: when I get free. In the muffled glow, in the slow, solitary motions of the night, I sat, listening, as their voices blended into one monotone that gradually died away in sleep.

Nine

Time and again I listen to the wind in the flues, hear the panes shake in the creaking frames, the sudden crack on the third tread of the stair, the start of fright as the door slams open and the deep voice growls its untoward, unwarranted command. Who can ever measure the fearsome effects of this power of negation? Little by little, cell by cell, formed in the blood and bone and skin and muscle and nerve tissue, this unnerving, fatal yielding? Time and again I goad myself into going on regardless, stiffening my resistance, urging myself to gather myself together again against this old enemy. Back. Back. To those Sunday afternoons in the Nissen hut where the teacher forever unfurls the great leathery-winged serpent that casts its mighty shadow across the place of desolation and the midget pilgrim hoists his weary burden. But no man ever went on this journey. This is the missing dimension, this dreadful absence of confidence that is like a sickness eating at the heart of resolution. Time and again I gird myself for the struggle, telling myself I need arm myself only with the truth. But what is the truth? Time and again I ask myself these questions. Am I doing this right? As if there is an authority to which I must submit my own self. As if there is a model I must follow. As if I have somehow lost the pattern, the set of guide-lines that might have led me in the right direction, to the proper conclusion. But there is no right and wrong of it. This is my story. The story of my self.

History conspires in the process of mystification. The time of austerity – it is ten years since the war ended – gives place to a period of local prosperity, whose material effects – television sets, washing machines, refrigerators – affect the face of ordinary life without inducing a radical change. The very idea of vast change seems to have evaporated; or, rather, it has been replaced by a goal that my people would have called betterment – a slow and gradual lifting of the individual by easy stages. My journey forward and upward will be by way of university. A newspaper, the posh newspaper that has been ordered specially to improve my chances of self-improvement, lies outspread upon the counterpane. Its language is too dense and allusive for my family to read, difficult for me, suggesting a range of potentialities that lie outside my experience, hinting at an infinitely complex web of social contingencies. The newspaper bridges the gulf between the realm of ideas and the real world. It seems to promise that there is a reality where ideas not only have currency but are taken for granted. It is for this reason that the notion of going to university becomes suffused in a mist of speculation. Let it be soon – I pray – let it be soon that I find myself in a room with colour-washed walls, pictures, apple-blossom in a stone jar, books, kindred spirits; let it be soon; and fall into a day-dream in which the very word colour-washed – culled perhaps from some magazine story, its brides in muslin, its pies in glaze – lulls, as with the motion of water, the sensation of light on water, apple-green, apple-cool, twigs breaking into bud, a drift of petals, pages ruffled by a warm wind, a friend – is he the one? – and all this, let it be soon.

To my father the university figured as a glorified school, where a training would take place for the professions, if only one could pass through the right hoops to get there. In this respect he was more sophisticated than most of the people in our streets, who either ignored this possibility or saw it as something far out of reach of our kind. My notion of studenthood was derived from the one or two Russian novels I had read in which the student appears as a soulful figure given to garrets, starveling passions and contemplation. At school I was assured that this life would be eminently suitable for me. I imagined entering into a community of like minds, where at last I should come into my own and feel at home. But how was a lecture different from a class, or a professor from a teacher? And on what basis, given that variations exist between one place and another, could I be expected to choose? What exactly was a university if it was not a school? All I really knew was that going away to college would give me a pretext to leave home, a home that was kind, clean, congenial, but in which I felt buried, cut off from my fellows, and where I lived in a state of suspended animation. And just as the library, that dark, quiet place, was to be a haven, a place of dim romantic aspiration, so I looked forward to going

142

away to college during these last months as to a bourne, where, no longer under surveillance, I would become my own person. I did not allow myself to be entered for the open examinations to the older universities, because there was a fee to find and I could not face the struggle to exact a new sum from the family funds – as I had done with the Italian trip – nor the shame of exposure as a fool in my father's eyes if I were to fail. Thus, though I was put into the special group with the other cleverer girls, it was purely to make up the numbers. The significance of that omission did not really impinge, since I had not yet understood the society in which I was contending for a place.

Meanwhile, however, history spawns horrors. The newspaper lies open on the counterpane. I sprawl on the floor, clutching my stomach, sick at heart. I cannot look at the newsprint again. A pit of bones. The words burn into my brain. A chamber of death. A hundred. A thousand. Tens of thousands. Millions. Such numbers cannot be encompassed. The illumination is sudden as flakes of lightning, and as dire: one livid instant that reveals the cesspit of the human heart. An attendant in a white coat is giving a cake of soap to an old lady. She is naked, spindle-shanked, her loose flanks dropping in folds of empty skin that lap her like a tired old garment. In her palm the soap is a little tablet of cement, a placebo intended to allay her suspicion that all is not well. Can this be true? Instantly I know that this is true. It is beyond invention. My father is weeping at the kitchen table. Where can I run to hide? Who will tell me that this is false? I retch tasting bile. I swill out my mouth with water, but there is no cleansing. I want to die rather than face these facts, but I am not brave; my father's blade is in the bathroom cabinet wrapped in its slip of oiled paper, but I am incapable of hurting one hair of my own head. I tell myself that I am good. I am not part of this monstrous humanity. I am not, nor could I ever be, an attendant in a white coat, doling out death to an old woman. But how can I live with this sacrifice? I want to run outside into the street and scream for help, but the street breathes quietly, its chimneys smoking, its children playing, a man with a cart weighing potatoes into a swatch of newspaper, while the blinkered horse munches, its great plashings steaming softly in the afternoon air, where long ago my grandmother used to run with a spade and carry the droppings to spread on her little square of dirt.

My grandmother lies in a vast urban cemetery under a green mound without a headstone. Not far away there are paupers' graves, grey

143

rounded slabs upended, leaning drunkenly in the weather, carved on both sides, memorials not so much of those dead people as of the epidemics that obliterated them at the turn of the century. Seven cars followed the hearse, a huge procession, followed on foot by the children of the family, myself and the cousins, who stood watching in the rain at a distance dictated in advance by our elders, lest we be troublesome. Afterwards we watched them straggle back to the cars, footing it through the long tousled grass, stumbling in the miry ground, the fathers helping the women; the weeping, the black umbrellas; and then the diggers, shovelling in the dirt, subsoil that was full of big stones and hunks of clay. I went and asked one of the men whether they were planning to give her an angel, or a marble book, or just one of the little low walls with the loops of pointy chains that reminded me of the crown of thorns. Depends what you pays, the man said, wielding his smeared spade like a weapon as he attacked the clods.

Easiest to set these evils together as part of the human condition: poverty, ignorance, death – a trinity of disasters so closely interfused that it is possible to evade any form of amelioration, to call alteration mere tinkering, a staving off of an inevitable doom. This fatalism, in my family and that whole great class of working people to which they belonged, produces a kind of mass inertia that stifles the will to change. Instead, they proceed along their allotted grooves with a stoic fortitude, with – even – a sense of good fortune. Hunger is just next door. Hunger is only yesterday. Now is the time. Now, when work is plentiful, when their labour brings in rewards and their children are promised the good life. Thus they buy me the newspaper, but when I try to discuss these issues my father, impatient of my finicky conscience, shouts: Nothing changes.

One night, a neighbour, an insurance man, calls to sell us a policy. The business is new to him and the sales patter sits clumsily on his tongue. He has had many jobs in the ten years since the war, when as an iron founder he worked in a protected industry. He has a fat wife and a fat, mentally defective daughter, who at the age of fourteen complained of a pain in her stomach and, to everybody's scandalised astonishment, was immediately delivered, without any assistance, of a fat baby. My mother makes tea and he sits at the table, explaining the terms to my father, who listens shrewdly, aware that there might be a snare in any salesman's talk. At length the deal is settled and I try to concentrate on my work as their conversation strays into money

144

matters in general and the state of the economy in particular. My mother pulls a face. There is something repellent in the man's posture of being in the know. He is ugly, completely bald, with a skull that resembles the knobbed head of a walking stick. Later my mother will grumble: Why bring that man into the house, sneaking round – as if we hadn't enough to do with our money? All of a sudden I hear him announce: Hitler was right. *What did you say*? The question slips out of my mouth before I have time to bite it back: *What did you say*? My cheeks burn. My mother nervously sets down a cup she is drying and puts a finger warningly to her lips. My father frowns. Interruptions are not allowed. Surprised, the man looks at me insolently and defiantly, my heart thundering, I stare back instead of retreating behind a cowed smile. There is a silence. The atmosphere affects the man, whose confidence ebbs and who replies almost diffidently: Hitler had the right idea – only his methods were wrong. I find it difficult to control my voice, which sounds thin and shrill in my own ears. How dare you, I squeak, how dare you suggest such a thing? My father says angrily: What do you know? I can tell he is bitterly ashamed of me for speaking out of turn. I say faintly: What about the war? In the past both my parents have remarked that this man never went to the war, and stayed at home lining his pockets, but my mentioning it here is a breach of courtesy. My father says scathingly: What do you know about the war? The insurance man shrugs: We should have been on their side. I say: That's fascism. My father roars: Keep your nose out of this, you! My mother protests: I'm surprised at you, letting me down. Apologise or leave the room at once. Don't mind me, says the man, I know what it's like: I've a girl of my own in the house.

For a moment, fearful of what would ensue when the man left the house, I struggled to say I was sorry, then I fled to my bedroom. I hated the man. I hated my parents' complaisance. I hated the impertinence of the parallel between myself and his idiot daughter. I felt sorry for the girl, but in my eyes the distance between us was immense: to me she seemed grotesque. The baby had been taken away from her and put into a home, and the man had asked for the girl to be sterilised, an incidental connection with the tales of horror that endowed him – and his money matters – with a peculiar nastiness that brought it all home: how it could all happen. Of course, it was all true. History was inescapable. It had all happened and in some form or another, given the nature of humanity, was bound to happen again and again until the world ended in that final atrocity – the ultimate war – the probability of which, long emblazoned in prophetic works that lent their own solemn testimony to the inevitable, and newly realised in banner headlines throughout the long cold war, gave to ordinary existence that sense of living on the lip of a sleeping crater, into which at any moment we might all be spilled, tipped by the slightest aberration in the balance of power, over which no single person could exercise the least influence, and which, equally, no person could escape. On the contrary, as presidents and peasants, rich and poor, men, women, every race, every colour, as each and every one was to be consumed, there was even a kind of majestic justice in that levelling, a lurid finality that bestowed on the books of doom – those avenging angels, those lakes of flame – the oppressive authority of a divine intention.

One day my Greek teacher drew a picture of the Parthenon and wrote underneath: the cradle of civilisation. The intimacy of those lessons made it possible to ask the question. Because, she said proudly, they invented every aspect of our culture: democracy, politics, oratory, tragedy, comedy, the art of rhetoric, philosophy . . . What is politics? I asked. She smiled. Her big soft lips trembled with laughter: Surely you can tell me? Politics means of those things concerning the city. But what is party politics? One must ask oneself, she murmured, whether it is proper that the city should be governed for the benefit of the many or whether on the contrary it exists for the advancement of the few? Surely, I said, it must be for the many? Sphinx-like, she smiled again. Schooling was supposed to encourage the free play of ideas but to avoid the promulgation of policies. Unaware of this awkward ambiguity, I tried to make her express a view – in vain. After all, she countered, the Greeks had their slaves. She offered me knowledge as the one great good. Yet as my eyes began to be opened to the evils of the world I agitated for instant solutions. I began to evolve a simple egalitarianism that owed more to metaphysics than to politics and that could be fitted together with other areas of learning to make a whole system. I wanted the lessons of the Bible and the Greek philosophers to be applied to the world in which I found myself. I wanted to believe in the primacy of reason, in the appeal to reason, in the ultimate triumph of reason. I imagined, moreover, that amongst the educated classes this state of reasonable intercourse had already come to pass, and that it lay in waiting for me just beyond the street corner. That whenever I managed to escape it would be there, intangibly, in the space between myself and people of like mind. I envisioned a future in which men and women, equally endowed, would treat each other with respect. Together, we would extend this ideality to include all mankind at home and abroad.

The gentlemen who interviewed me at the first university could not have been more different from our insurance collector. They were three in number, all venerable. Each one in turn questioned me about my reading and my interests. To me they seemed themselves like creatures out of books – seasoned, intricately described, the waistcoat buttons, the stroked whiskers, the probing eyes that looked upon my vulnerability with a benign deliberation. When I told them that I wanted to be a journalist, they shared with me a kindly disdain; it was the first time I had come across the notion that to be a reporter was not a dignified profession. I believed them implicitly and at once consigned the press to the dustbin, preferring the stately condescension of these academics to what, they implied, must be adjudged the brash company of ephemeral prose. In this way, because I was extremely impressionable, while opening one door to me, they closed another all unwittingly; or, rather, they failed to recognise the extent of their influence, and while professing perfect disinterestedness were none the less quite blatantly coercive. Two authors were mentioned. The professor with the pipe lit a leisurely match and bit the curved black stem, sucking the flame into the bowl. Virginia Woolf? Ah, he chuckled, a pretty stylist. Then, *Sons and Lovers*, Lawrence was just then coming into vogue with the critics. Who is the real villain of that story? The other men smiled reassuringly, waiting for me to fall into the trap. Baffled, I stared from one to the other, seeking for clarification. Outside, the snow was falling on a thorny red bush, whose spines squeaked maddeningly against the glass. Sensing that this was the wrong reply, my heart beat very rapidly as I stammered: The father. The first man smiled broadly, delightedly, saying: Come now. Another, younger man studied my face carefully, compassionately, aware of my discomfiture, while the speed of my heart-beat took away my breath and the power of speech. There was no space for thought. Surely they were mistaken? But the possibility of challenging their verdict was a million miles away. How could I tell them about the smell of new bread cooling under a cloth or convince them that the father, clomping into the kitchen with his eternal egotism, was the real villain? Or even, that the very notion of simple villainy was a false trail, a moral judgement that left too much out of the reckoning to be of any use at all. Think of the title, the man says, cajolingly, the sons destroyed by the mother-love. I lick my dry lips, nodding, lying tacitly, because my own life is on the line. I need these men. The snow melts against the glass, settling in soft irregular masses in the webbed bush. My hands are clammy, clenched. My knees tremble. I have a great deal to say, but I listen, my lips sealed. Out there, are the silent multitudes. I belong to them and one day I shall speak to them in my own voice. How do you feel about joining us here? the man says. Politely I falter: I should love to come. He rises, putting out a paternal hand for me to shake, ending the interview. And we should love to have you, he says, ushering me out into the corridor, where – alone again – I press my burning forehead against a notice-board and pretend to read the lists until I have recovered my stunned wits.

On the train going home I feel bruised, out of sorts, in spite of this evident success. Their very mannerisms, that air of gallantry extended to female students, as if they were handling fragile goods with especial delicacy, enforced its own peculiar response: like a puppet on a stick, I dangled, displaying my wits, my neat little tricks, and concealing my real reservations; gained a place, but failed then – or thereafter – to achieve any reciprocity. Of course they were bound to want me: I was a good girl. A good learner. The train passes through a landscape transformed by snow, black and white, diagrammatic, and yet desolate, its beauty unable to anneal the sense of lives laid to waste in pit villages, in mill towns, in vast urban sprawls. What they saw was an able student, a charming young woman, a good girl. The rest was invisible. Of course, because my conduct was well-advised, since to confront would have seemed inappropriate, improper, out of place. Yet I feel compromised. I suspect that there is a price to be paid for the privilege of batting received ideas back and forth: already it has set me apart. I belong nowhere. I tell myself I am heading for the promised land. From this vantage point – on a train that flies northwards with the scudding wind through the mute hutched houses, row after parallel row, it seems that I am about to ride to freedom on the backs of people, whose labour is scarcely even recognised, let alone under-stood. In a few years' time even their labour will have lost its value; and though I do not know this as a fact, I sense this decline as a latent threat, so that my own emancipation will seem , in the end, to be a kind of treason.

In the buffet car a man insinuates himself into my company. The truth is, I cannot resist making conquests. My facility in the art of flirtation never fails to excite me. I smile and conciliate, and this attracts the man. He is some kind of small executive – portly, dapper and self-important. He thinks he is a fine fellow. A short bout of nonsensical conversation is in order before I declare myself: archly, I inform him that I am an anarchist. But the man is too stupid or besotted by drink for gallantry, because to whatever I assert in the way of principle he merely titters: Measles. Idealism, he proclaims, like measles, is a childish ailment. But as I persist he stops trying to keep my knees between his own thighs under the table and gets red in the face, and angry, shouting in a boorish way again and again: Measles. Eventually, ashamed of my craving for attention, I escape back to my compartment, vowing that I will never outgrow these ideas: beauty, truth, goodness, equality, freedom. Never would I allow this business-man to triumph over me by letting myself lapse into impotence. Never again would I succumb to the forces of despair. I longed to perform some act of mighty heroism, to prove myself worthy of these words and to tell the world that all need not be lost. What could I do? The train rocked noisily, pursuing its predictable course. I listened. If only I could even sort out the meaning of that music, it might be something. Rattlings and shuttlings, rockings and tiny abrupt shocks that shuddered along its moving parts. I stood in the corridor where two carriages were conjoined, staring at the couplings that writhed and jerked constantly like some animal in pain, afraid even to tread on that infirm ground – afraid on the train, exposed in my solitariness; panicked on the platform, when I lost my ticket only to find it instants later tucked inside my glove. Alone, I was nothing. What compromises would I not in the end make to attach myself to the safety of some anchorage?

At the fag-end of the journey, on the tram in my own town, precariously balanced, as if madness was always just around the next bend, the images revolving in my head shifted me ceaselessly from elation to despair and back again: that seductive study, warm with tobacco smoke and old books with gold-.ooled spines and vanilla-coloured paperbacks; my father insisting on taking me to the train, making himself late for work, trudging through the sludgy streets with old socks over our shoes to keep them dry, me to be smart for the interview, he for the factory, because it would be cold underfoot if the floor got puddled; the probing intruder in the dusty dark when the news reel shows soldiers dropping long ago and far away on the Russian front, men and machines, black and white, men dropping, dropping like a trail of litter across a vast frozen field; my grandmother coming from Ginny's house the day of the funeral with a shopping bag full of coal, and on her knees, the tears streaming down her cheeks, arranging the chunks on a lattice-work of wood chips, piece by gleaming piece. I sob aloud and put my hand across my mouth, pretending to cough, but nobody notices. The faces of my fellow-travellers stare dumbly out of the tram-car windows. I want to cry: Unite! But naturally I do nothing of the sort, and a few minutes later I pick my way very carefully through the slush so as not to spoil my new brown shoes.

At this time I became increasingly aware of the gap between the ideal and the real worlds. Afraid that any action could have deplorable consequences, I began to adopt passivity as a possible alternative to guilt. I cultivated the art of not doing. As a first stage I gave up reading the newspaper, which had in any case been discredited by the academics. The less I knew, the less I was likely to be at fault. If, when I came of age, I refused to vote, I could not be held responsible. But when I put forward this view in those daily discussions that formed the staple diet of our lunch-time saunterings about the school, other girls were not slow to point out that only the dead can truly to be said to have the attribute of neutrality. And as we strolled, euphoric, arm-in-arm along the drive-way where the beech hedge once more uncurled its limp soft foliage out of pointed copper casings, fired with a desire to prove my own nobility of soul, I strove to express to these girls – prefects on the watch lest little girls heedlessly trample the shrubberies – the virtues of passive resistance. Most of the youths I knew were deferring their compulsory military service until after their studies, but one or two went abroad, and one refused on conscientious grounds. His pacifism was questioned. He was taken to a tribunal, won his case and eventually he was permitted to work in a hospital. I longed for an opportunity to demonstrate my own high principles, but as a girl I was not expected to do military service. There were no opportunities for heroism. I could only make assertions, which, because no sacrifice was expected of me, could only seem hollow. Moreover, far from producing tranquillity of soul, such conversations left me boiling with a rage to do something, so that our arrangements – to go swimming after school, or shopping in town on Saturday afternoon, our ardent deliberations in the best department store over the choice between two shades of lipstick, two fents of cotton found bundled into a bargain box, two café tables, two kinds of sandwich, each tantalisingly lying on a paper napkin on a silver platter with wisps of cress – were informed by a sense of their essential absurdity: these delightful diversions were merely stumbling-blocks, snares and delusions in the way of truth.

On Sunday mornings I lie in bed late, plotting subversion. I have decided that it behoves me to make a stand on principle against going to church. For several weeks nothing happens. At last, one evening, the vicar called at the back door. My mother always hurried him through the kitchen as quickly as possible into the front room. She signalled me to follow with the tea-tray. When I went in with the tea, my mother was looking uncomfortable. The vicar was a big, shy man, who had no aptitude for conversation. Flushed, his face looked like a great bag of blood that was about to burst. When he was praying or uttering the words of the services, his voice cracked and trembled with reverence. For the first time I noticed he had scarcely any eyebrows. A thick, crooked vein throbbed in his temple. I wondered whether my mother had asked him to take me to task for not going to church. It seemed unlikely. She had let me lapse almost absentmindedly, with no fuss, yet here, looking grave and agitated, was the vicar. We have not seen you in church, he began. She's been revising, my mother fussed. Here was the opportunity to make a dignified stand. I muttered: I've decided not to come any more. I wanted him to recognise me as a thinking person. How I longed for a long and interesting theological discussion! But as I shambled through my explanation, his face seemed to swell with displeasure and even distress, until at length he said: You must pray for guidance. But how can I pray if I no longer believe? You must pray to be delivered from the sin of pride. I was about to protest my humility when my mother, who was looking very earnest and tearful, burst out: I think she's letting herself be influenced by these well-to-do friends. I demurred. Well, it's true, my mother went on, you told me yourself that none of them goes to church. The vicar hastily popped a couple of butterfly buns in his mouth, effectively silencing himself, while his eyes strayed hopefully to the tea-pot. Then he offered to pray for me; being prayed over aloud in the front room was horribly embarrassing. Eventually he left. I had made no promises and I never went to church again. Neither of my parents ever tried to persuade me to go, though my father did say: How come you know best when all these clever men think different?

It is much more uncomfortable at home than at church on Sunday mornings. I miss the serenity of the service. On the coldest of spring days my father insists on airing the house. It is one day of the week when his energy is put to house-work. He does the heavy jobs. He washes the windows and paintwork, cleans out the gutterings and gratings. He has no long ladder, and so, grunting with exertion, he has to sit on the upstairs window-sills in order to reach outside. He bangs open my bedroom door. I peep my nose out of the sheets and my breath freezes in clouds of vapour. I close my eyes, but he says: Here, hold my legs while I lean out. During these wet and draughty operations I have to play the handmaiden when I am at home. There is no question of lurking in bed for long. He battles about the house, calling for attention at every turn, while doors slam in the breeze. I am instructed to rinse out slimy rags. To polish door-knobs. To boil the milk and make a cup of coffee. Mid-morning, a retired work-mate always calls for coffee. He has an allotment and brings cabbage and lettuce and whatever flowers he can find for my mother. At the point when this old man is due to arrive, my father stops cleaning and orders me to fill the cups. Then I must wash the cabbage, searching carefully for soil and grubs before shredding it into the pan.

On a fine day I might sit on the top step to peel the potatoes in the sun. As the old man squeezes past me, he grumbles: You'll get piles if you sit on a cold stone. Mind you cut out all the eyes, my father shouts. His voice is warm, full of good-humour. When he first met the old man he was a boy of thirteen. The man taught him his trade and paid him his wage out of his own wages, and, being childless, made my father his family. As an honorary grandchild I receive a threepenny bit each birthday. The old man has large brown splotches on his weathered head, for now he has been free of the factory since before the war and spends all his time out of doors. He is thin, brittle and stick-like, and his thrift is legendary. If he asks for sixpence for the vegetables my father will give ninepence, at which the old man will add, with a sideways look: Then there's the blooms. They might be sweet-peas or Michaelmas daisies or marguerites. I arrange the flowers in a vase that has a pattern like a wizened face. I turn this face away from me automatically, though I am no longer afraid. I remember a time when I could not sit alone in the same room with the vase for fear that it would get me. I only half listen to the talk – How is Sammy? Sammy died. Did you see they got a rise in the Hoffman pressers? A rise . . . they never . . . I sniff the flowers. The strong daisy smell. The long narrow leaves. The allotment is one of dozens of strips redeemed from the hollows, which not so long ago had seemed like the real country with its thorn bushes and elderberries and which now I know is only a few acres of undeveloped land. I have begun to read a book by Proust in which a description of may-blossom begins by evoking the small speckled cups, the veiled creamy masses, with an aching accuracy that recalls exactly the marvel of seeing the hawthorns in flower for the first time; and then goes on for puzzling page after page which leaves me floundering, wondering: But what is the meaning of all this description? To what end? And why has this old man tilled this small oblong of soil all these long years? And where does my father get the will to wash away the grime from the paintwork every week? Everything is beginning to seem small. I feel that I am already becoming detached, not part of things. Thus I arrange the flowers. Thus I listen. But I feel cut off already and at a distance, as if I am enclosed in a glass shell. The old man says, with the faintest hint of disparagement: Well, you're a lucky girl to be kept at home so long. Knowing that he is deaf I shout: I'm going to university soon. My father flinches at this assertiveness: You mean you will if you make the grade.

To this end – always at the last possible time – I revise for the examinations. During warm spells I work in my bedroom and am never interrupted except by my mother who, with unfailing solicitude, brings me cups of coffee and bacon sandwiches and cake. Sometimes I let the coffee go cold by the open window, and specks of soot from the chimney fires settle on the skin. Once or twice on the very eve of the dreaded day I surreptitiously study right through the night. My habit of working at a very inferior level of concentration is abruptly jettisoned in favour of a fierce attack. In this way I finally find myself adequately but by no means perfectly prepared. During the hour or two before the test begins I feel sick: my head throbs and my bowels open – again and again. But once inside the silent room I read the questions and find myself instantly able to estimate the limits of my information. Writing the answers is a dry, cool, yet searching process. Mostly everything disappears that is beyond the tip of my pen and the half-page across which my hand flies; but now and again I hear the rustle of paper, a faint cough, foot-falls as a mistress in her academic gown softly billows between the rows of desks, while against windows set high in the panelled hall a light summer rain patters without cessation.

Out of these examinations we emerge elated and affectionate. Again we stroll about the grounds, lie on the big field, our open books reduced to the status of mere accessories, while once again we explore time, space, God, the dark cloud that sits on some far distant horizon and grows very quietly and secretly, almost overnight, as mushrooms do in moist, fertile ground. Shuddering, concluding that there is nothing we can do to avert this monstrous thing, we tell ourselves that we are the first generation for whom there may be no future.

And yet, of course, we talked constantly about our own future careers. On Friday mornings there had always been a long assembly at which an account would often be given of the worthy work of some former pupil. One girl would become a missionary, another a nurse; many would teach because, they said, it would fit in well with motherhood. Perhaps because my own mother had always worked I never thought of marriage as an occupation. Matrimony was not an alternative to a job, it was an inevitable outcome. In the mean time a sense of my own incompleteness, combined with ignorance, fear and dislike of the outside world, made a breeding ground for the passivity that I adopted as a standard of conduct; but because I expected that eventually I, too, would have to earn my living, I was constantly asking myself: Could I do that? Or that? Or that? To go to university would be to enter into a kind of limbo. Beyond would lie necessity. But in the interim there would be freedom, and freedom was simply the absence of control.

Meanwhile, between my father and myself, a miniature cold war was being waged. Going for the interviews had been only a preliminary skirmish, an engagement justified by me on the grounds that all girls were expected to make these rounds as a matter of routine. I knew without being told that my father was expecting me to live at home as a student. I had decided that I would go away. There was no discussion of this decision because I was afraid of eliciting an outright ban. Yet it would be difficult for me to go, not just because of his opposition, not just because it would tear the pattern of our life together, but because a vivid sense of danger constantly undermined my confidence. I knew that this danger was not physical, but mental; it was as if the plenitude of impressions put a strain on the imagination. I was dreadfully afraid that one day I would simply stop working like an over-wound clock. Sometimes I would lie in bed wondering whether I would ever be able to get up again. I would close my eyes and feel myself falling. Yet at the same time a terrible elation accompanies this sensation, for this is freedom, this loosening of control, this process of becoming finally detached.

During those last weeks I walked slowly slowly home from school. The desire to lie down and blot it all out was so impelling that I had to force my legs to make each move: along the main road on a path past a tram-track where grey-blue pebbles the size of goose eggs had been packed between the lines. Between the pebbles grass had sprouted in spring-time. Now it was brown and singed. In July great sycamores drooped their full-grown leaves. The husks of growing things made a thick pinkish dust on the ground. The tram would go racketing past, singing and swaying. The smell of hot metal. Then two or three mongrel dogs came trotting along the gutter, nose to tail, following their leader. Between the path and the tracks was a wire fence with posts of coarse cracked concrete. Walking, I muttered. The habit of talking, of taking note, of making a mention – now the spark as the cables snatch at each other in passing, now the sensitive lifting of the one front paw of the lame yellow dog as it drops on its haunches to rest before hobbling after the pack – took me over the same ground day after day, until the last day of school came and, with a very small gush of sentiment, I gave a final look at the den that was already grown over with thickly leaved new branches in the tall beech hedge.

In the long light evenings of late summer I go for solitary walks. Already the journey to school has assumed a retrospective glamour. I retrace the path from the street corner, down the main road, to the traffic lights, along past the tram-lines into the quiet suburban streets that are lined with trees and old walls. On rain-washed evenings I breathe in the coolness and the odour of moist stone. Dusk transforms the city, slowly sapping the colour, leaving only form and silhouette as if the roads and buildings are fashioned out of shadow and beaten lead, a muted gleaming, where underfoot in the thin film of wetness on the flags passing feet have pressed the first fallen leaves flat. The craving to make an impression, to fashion things my way, forces me out into the street. But where can I go? Who can I tell? I pass houses where the curtains have been left open after the lamps have been lit. I see a woman sitting alone at a table staring into a glass. A man raking the fire. A bedroom wall where a kite in the shape of a wide-winged dragon is pinned in haphazard flight. A black dragon like a fallen angel. A hallway with a smoky parchment shade. These separate images pass by silently, hinting at lives lived side by side, forever disjoined. I long to heal these divisions. I construct a perfect universe. I walk slowly, wanting to account for everything. But if I stand for even a moment at a street corner, looking both ways, a man comes and jostles beside me, peering into my face. I move off hastily, pretending not to notice, and a wordless jeer issues from his throat, like spew. Nervous now, hurrying, knowing that I have strayed from home too far, too late, I come to the school and discover that the iron gates are closed. On the day of leaving I did not cry. I try again to summon tears – in vain. Now I regret not taking my proper leave. Behind the hedges the building will be lonely without me. I want to steal one last look. By what law are these barricades erected? Why should I not enter now? With timid defiance I give the gate a shake. The caretaker who lives in the lodge-house knocks on the window and waggles an irate finger. Out of uniform, high-heeled and flounced, I offer my most beguiling smile. But he drops the curtain with an oblivious scowl, and seeing that he has already forgotten my face, I understand at last that I have left indeed. I feel very strange and precarious. I cannot get inside anything. There is a high impenetrable gloss on the surface of the world. I am in danger of falling off. I walk home very quickly, closing my eyes from time to time to feel myself falling.

Ten

The winds wakes me early. I hear it breaking against the house in beating waves. I listen. I think: This is the last day. Today I shall finish. The house is warm and – a rare day this – empty. I have a whole day to myself. I spread myself in the bed, luxuriating. But I cannot afford to waste a precious minute. Life is too short. I must be doing. I must get up at once. Dress. Eat. Hurry to the window. Sit myself down at the desk. Listen. The house is quiet, humming with silence. The wind is settling. In the garden the thinnest twigs twitch, but across the valley the wooded hills are motionless, flat and formal like painted scenery. Is this really me, sitting here, composed, composing myself? Distanced by years from my own old self, I remember the street and the time when I seemed to be nothing but bits and pieces, pierced, scattered, flying apart in a wind.

Now, as I come near the end, I spread out the local paper long and lovingly preserved by my mother amongst her keepsakes, in which the examination results are listed. It is the hottest day of the year. On the front page there is a picture of the open-air swimming pool, packed with people; the faded photograph has captured the rapturous open mouths of children splashing, recalling lunch-hours basking against the walls of the factory yard in a yellow sun-dress. The hot smell of sun on skin. Cat-calls and laughter as a youth attaches one end of a snaking hose to a fire-hydrant and the other to his fly-front while his mates, stripped to the waist, dance in the sudden spray of the makeshift fountain.

That summer, waiting for the results, I worked in the same shed as my father. The shed was simply one of a row of huge, barn-like structures, each of which housed some thousand people together with the machinery of their different trades. Why work, my father fumed, when you could be in the fresh air? Because I need things. What things? Aloud I say: Just clothes and things. Working is a mug's game. Only for a few weeks, I plead, till I get the things I need. In secret, aided by my mother, I began to tick items off the list: home-made sheets from my Lancashire aunt with a slight defect in the bottom right-hand corner; embroidered pillow-slips from Ginny's mother; six apostle-spoons from the old man of the allotment carefully lapped in a pink georgette handkerchief that had belonged to his wife; from my youngest aunt's damp cellar my grandmother's trunk, its brown leatherette crusted white with mildew. And out of my own earnings, my first pair of coloured shoes, a wicked peacock blue to match a floating coat that has wide sleeves that buckle at the wrists.

The paper is soft and sallow with age, coming apart in the creases. A Yorkshireman of indomitable character and herculean achievements is honoured for his contributions to philosophy. On Salisbury Plain soldiers in a simulated atomic explosion are told the message is: Dig or die. Princess Margaret sprains an ankle and limps at her twenty-fifth birthday party, where at the suggestion of the Duke of Edinburgh steaks are carved from one of a fine herd of Aberdeen Angus on the Balmoral estate. At the Geneva conference Sir Anthony Eden is described as a rock, and President Eisenhower claims that the Americans are on a crusade of peace. In France troops are mobilised to send to Algeria, while in Kenya two British police officers are sentenced to eighteen months' hard labour for torturing a Kikuyu prisoner to death, after first manacling him in an indescribable position. An IRA bomb warning is called a hoax in the poorest taste. Major General Roscoe C. Wilson comments to the press that US servicemen prefer British brides because they are home-loving and enjoy housework. A man murders his wife and baby by knocking them on the head with a hammer before spending the evening at the theatre. Four schoolboys are charged with the theft of firearms from a Combined Cadet Force armoury. At a conference on criminology, held in an airy flower-decorated hall at Bedford College for women, a psychiatrist provokes laughter when he remarks that he has only ever met one murderer who was normal. The closure of two large cotton mills in Lancashire is threatened. At the county court a man and woman are each fined ten pounds for neglecting their five children. In Blackpool a committee of veterans complain that the cenotaph is being desecrated by cricket, football, picnics, sunbathing and amorous dalliance.

Back. The water pools in the yard in rivulets that are rainbowed with oil, running irregularly between the crushed cinders. Girls scream in protest and a wooden-faced commissionaire turns off the tap as the siren whines, reminding me of the heap of bedding under the stairs and the sound of planes droning away in the distance like a swarm of bees. I sit out of doors till the last possible moment, the paper unfolded on the step to protect my yellow dress. Starched and clean and gleaming as the yellow yolk of an egg. My name is in print for the very first time. It is all coming true. Yet I feel angry. At the thought of the five abused children crawling about amongst the trodden remnants of food, the smeared heaps of excrement, I feel angry: but what can I do? The idea of my own impotence is a knife that severs the feeling as it starts to shoot into life. I cultivate a numbing indifference. Yet something – the root of all being, all knowing – is constantly growing inside of me, reviving inside of me. So that I wake mornings, even then, those limpid mornings, bursting with joy, expecting the miracle. Love is the great redeemer. Love is the saving grace.

Every morning I walked to work with my father. Come along, come along, he would chivvy, you don't want to get quartered. Going in and coming out there were the clocking machines. A minute late and a quarter of an hour's pay would be docked off the wages. As a booking clerk I worked by a conveyor belt, taking off bundles of cloth, tearing one strip of paper off a docket and returning the bundle to the belt. All around there were sections doing different tasks, each one more or less simple in operation. Each routine was perfectly monotonous and unpolluted by the need for thought. A robot could have sufficed to do most tasks, and in due course this improvement would take place with a consequent loss of jobs. But at that time unemployment was not a grave issue. I was far more occupied by a sense of the tedium of these tasks than by economic questions about what might happen if the work supply failed. The place was light, warm and airy, but the noise of machinery and the monotony was insufferable. It was impossible to talk except in the breaks. Indeed, since most people were on piece work there was little incentive to indulge in conversation. It was necessary to work hard all the time in order to make a living. Somebody like me who was not involved in production but merely in shunting the work from one section to the next and who was paid by the hour could afford spells of rest between rushes of work, but these were relatively short and were almost harder to bear than working, since there was then nothing to occupy the minutes.

That summer a neighbour of ours, a frail old Jew, was dying. Having survived two heart-attacks and several bouts of pneumonia, he had become blind and was visited frequently by relations who wanted to put him in a home. In the sweltering evenings of the heat-wave my mother took him home-made lemonade and volunteered me to read. It never failed to surprise me that a house that looked like all the rest on the outside should be so foreign inside. Uncle Levy lay on a sofa against fat sausage pillows with tassels that came straight out of the Arabian nights. Close to hand on one side there was a black and red inlaid cabinet in which lived innumerable tiny silver chairs and tables, and on the other a dresser covered in a beaded cloth with a biscuit box full of dry macaroons, two wine glasses, a decanter full of Madeira and a skull-cap, which he wore only when I was reading out of the Bible. His head was flattish on top, with a long, thick, sleek slab of hair; his skin was livid, bloodless; and his lips were faintly blue, transparent and lined. My mother would push me in through his back door, crying: Hello, love, she's here again. Reading was the easy part, but of this he would quickly tire. His hand would push the air away very gently to tell me to stop and he would want me to talk, and when I stopped talking, he would catch hold of my wrist or my fingers with his own weak fingers to prevent me from going. Stay and talk to my young man, he quavered, the son of my sister's son.

The young man is a student. Bending over the bed to kiss the old man's cheek, he radiates energy, health, well-being. He brings a dish of cold jellied fish in a glass jar – gefilte fish from his mother – and a Yiddish newspaper, which he reads with difficulty. How are you? As you see, I am dying. He waves us away. Talk, he says, talk to each other. You are both young. Reluctant, drawn, I say: I must go. Tell me how he looks, the old man yearns. Does he look well? He looks very well, I say politely, but a bit sunburned on the nose. The student's eyes light up with laughter. She is a good girl, says Uncle Levy, when her mother brought her home from the hospital my old woman – may her soul rest in peace – was the first one to give her a kiss.

I go into the scullery and make tea. There is no stove, only two gas rings at the side of the sink. The oil-cloth on the floor has worn in holes and the coconut matting at the door is frayed. While I stir the pot, breathing in the fragrant steam, the student lounges in the doorway, watching me work with one of those singular smiles that tells me the miracle is about to happen. My heart gives a lurch. Within a few minutes – at first sight – I fall in and out of love. What are you going to read at university? he asks. The form of the question is unfamiliar. Books, I say. He gives a great shout of laughter. Teasing, he says: What sort of books? Incapable of answering, I pour out the tea. He comes and stands close beside me. He is wearing a large, shapeless jumper. He puts his hands on my shoulders and turns me round till we are facing each other. I catch a faint waft of something aromatic – talcum powder, or lotion, or tooth-paste mingled with the odour of washed wool. As my confidence ebbs, he seems to gain ground. Very rapidly, within the space of these few moments, I fall in and out of love again and again, so that by the time he leaves I am trapped in a complication of feelings, a web of wanting and not wanting.

Now, as I waited for the evenings and the possibility that the student would call again, the days seemed very long. There were no windows in that place, only skylights high up in which there was frosted glass, so that not even the clouds were visible. The outlets were guarded. These features heightened the sense of being cut off, incarcerated, in a zone where time seemed to stand still. Like everybody else I soon learned to measure out my days into four shorter spells: between clocking in and break, between break and lunch, between lunch and tea, between tea and clocking out. Very soon I too listened longingly for the sound of the tea trolley. Whether standing or sitting on a high buffet, leaning and lifting was aching work and I craved the chance to change positions, to have the free use of my own limbs, to squat on a ledge or walk about and stretch. At break-times my father called me across to sit with him and bought me a chocolate biscuit from the trolley. From time to time he said to people: This is my girl. Sometimes, anxious to make sure people did not imagine I was permanent, he even went on to say: She's going to the university after a few weeks. Just as he had not at first liked the idea of my mother going out to work, so he felt uneasy about his daughter being in the factory. Yet because factory work had always been held up to me as an example of the worst possible fate, it was a relief to be there. To know for myself was better than not to know. To be inside the factory at last was to see an ordered world that was saner than the threatened horrors, but also more inexorable, representing, in some way, the triumph of reason over human qualities that were both more anarchic but also, perhaps, no less important. Perhaps because I was older, the logic of the factory was easier to understand than the logic of school, but it was no less inhumane. It was a tread-mill again. Over and over again I revolved in my mind the realisation that there seemed to be no justice in this arrangement of things. The precepts by which my childhood had been guided – notions of honour and fairness – seemed to exist merely as convenient parts of an arbitrary system. It seemed wrong that such a mass of people should be condemned into a penal confinement simply because they had been born without advantages.

In the absence of telephones and cars, the only means of communication was on foot. Each evening I waited for the student to call. Then, shamelessly abandoning the old man to his pensive couch, we retreated to the back yard to sit on the doorstep in the long smouldering evenings of the heat-wave, where more or less under surveillance our melancholy romance ripened in the waning sun. Now and then my mother came out into our own yard, making excuses: to water the snap-dragons or to nip off the dead-heads. There was no question of our being allowed to go out together, no future in this relationship at all. The old man was sinking fast. When he died, that would be the end.

But in spite of this impossibility we began to meet. Sometimes, instead of coming to visit, he asked me to go for a walk. Soon we were both going away, but in the mean time he had the ability to make these meetings seem imperative. Nobody had ever imposed himself with such urgency – except my father. The temptation to sink myself into this new subjection was physical or emotional but never total. Sometimes it seemed to me our relationship had no real content to it at all except his attack and my defence. And yet the longer the tussle lasted, the more inextricably involved I became.

Sometimes we walked towards the centre of the city, penetrating the inner circle, where already bull-dozers were obliterating the maze of streets in which for little more than a century our grandparents and our great grandparents had spent their labour and their lives. Belonging, like me, to the outer fringes of this district, he wanted no part of this coming change. We walk hand in hand across tracts of vacant ground on pavements no longer flanked by walls. We stand on the edge of desolation where the builders have posted warnings: Keep Out Keep

Out Keep Out. Beyond the wire fence a disembowelled house is ready to collapse; in an upstairs room a fireplace hangs suspended, its tiles patterned with vine-leaves. He says: I am going to live in the holy land. His mother and father are against this new exodus. He says: I am going to the promised land. I listen, finding it hard to understand. Does he really believe in the words? The bow of burning gold? The arrows of desire? Yes, yes, he tells me, a thousand times yes. Already there are lemon groves in the valleys and olive trees on the hills.

Sometimes we go the other way. Daring, I take off my sandals and walk barefoot on grass verges that are deliciously damp with dew. I imagine that we are living together in one of the brick villas. In the gardens – a trellised arch, a pathway bordered by blue lobelia, a bed of roses, roses of Sharon, milk and honey, a heap of white wheat, twin roes, myths and music and unspeakable delight – people talk to each other across fences, glancing at us incuriously as we slowly saunter past. And as we walk, his words flood into my mind. My own comments – uncertain, sceptical, timid – punctuate the flow of his thought, provoking an irascible reaction on his part that is not altogether unlike the quick scorn of my father. But he is often mockingly tender. He hooks his arm round my neck and whispers again and again: What are you thinking? This gesture, this question, scatters my thoughts. I try to collect myself together. Bending at the kerb to put on my sandals I pick up a heart-shaped leaf from a lilac bush; already there is a spot of decay near the base of the stem. Twirling the leaf I say: But surely wherever you go it will be the same. How? What is needed, I begin, what is needed . . . Annoyed, he shrugs. He says: Why are you always fiddling with things?

Once we went boating on Waterloo lake, where my father had tried unsuccessfully to teach me to row. At night, even more than by day, I was afraid of the water. He rowed right across the deep dark centre of the lake to the far-off lonely shore that was screened by trailing willows. The boat wobbled as he stood and urged me to climb out on to the bank. The grass was heavy-headed with seed and drenched with dew. Using his knee, he tried to force me to my knees. Deeply embarrassed, I murmured: No, I'll get wet. In the boat he drew me into his arms and kissed me on the throat, the neck, the shoulders, the mouth. Terrified that the least movement would tip us into the water I held myself rigid, until, sighing, he finally took up the oars again. Of course I was afraid in those pre-pill days of what might happen, but I was far more afraid of being late home. Staying out with him until the early hours, I would creep into the house, slotting my latch-key silently into the lock, only to hear my father shouting at me: Do you call this a decent time? I must go, I kept saying, I must go. When are you going to get yourself emancipated? he raved. Nothing happened. He kept urging me to liberate myself, which meant to accept a new bondage. Still nothing happened. Naturally he grew bored and, to punish me, stopped calling. I continued to read to the old man, whose blind, nerveless hands now and then strayed almost absent-mindedly over my knees, seeking the hem of my skirt, at which he plucked with little moans of pleasure. I pushed my chair out of reach and accepted a small glass of bitter-sweet wine. My whole being concentrated on willing his nephew to come. Then, very late, when the sun was already setting, bathing the walls of the street in a fugitive red glow, he would suddenly be there. Incapable of saying no, risking bumping into my father as he was coming home from the track, I would go and – having nowhere else to go – we would wander once again round the streets. When night-fall came we clung to each other in shop doorways. But still nothing happened. Always, mindful that I was a good girl, mindful of his own mission, it was he that brought an end to these fluctuating encounters. Relieved of this oppression, split, I dragged myself away only to begin plotting at once how we would meet again.

One day as I sat by my father with my mug of tea, he said to me: They are not like you. I was startled. I realised I must have spoken aloud. The echo of my own question remained in my head: how can they bear it every day, day after day, year in, year out? There were only four women on my section: two were my age or younger; one was a married woman; one was a woman close to retirement who had worked there for nearly fifty years. These women spoke freely about their lives and private affairs. Mostly, they talked about money, about making ends meet. It was easy to tell from their talk that it was not stupidity that had condemned them to this kind of servitude. The youngest girl of all swore constantly, displayed huge bruises on her neck and breasts and complained that her boy-friend was a brute: if he tries to do it to me again, she would scoff, I'll stick a bloody knife in his back-side, next time he's not looking. I say: What exactly do you do together? Offended, the girl turns her back on me. According to my youngest aunt who also worked in the same shed, my father kept me near him to prevent me from hearing this kind of talk. She liked me to take my break near her bench. She would sometimes come to fetch me. Then she would whisper: Take off your overall so that everybody can see your pretty dress. And again, as we walked past a knot of forewomen, in an undertone: See there, we call them the unholy trinity – the witch, the worm and the weasel. Then aloud, she would cry: This is my sister's girl. Once she warned: I've seen you, making up to that Levy lad. We are just friends, I say. All the same, be careful you don't get used. Aloud, I say to my father: Why do all these people let themselves be used? My father always hated speculative questions. He said irritably: They are not the same as you. How? They are used to it, that's how. They are just ignorant women. Pay no attention.

My father distinguished between proper women like my mother and the rest. So far as he was concerned, I fitted into neither category: I was something between a child, a part of himself like an extra limb, an idea in his own mind, and a highly prized possession of which he was shyly proud. Occasionally I joined him on the way home from work. Each evening, as thousands of people were released by the siren, what looked like a mob quickly dispersed, for they were all rushing to resume their real lives. Sometimes there were fights, but more often this progress was orderly, though hectic. My father always walked with a number of his work-mates at a great speed. The noise of the machinery meant that they talked loudly and gesticulated a great deal. But they were skilled men, highly respected, an élite group. When I was allowed to speak, they listened judicially and were pleased that I noted that the conditions of work were exacting. If I seemed sensible, my father beamed. Sometimes, wanting to be gracious, one of the men would say: She's a beautiful speaker. Then, I would be overwhelmed with happiness at being found creditable. At other times the owner of the factory walked round his domain. On these perambulations he was always flanked by a bevy of managers and under-managers, vying to reach his ear. He was a small, insignificant-looking man, a millionaire, a philanthropist, one who was mentioned in the newspapers and had sat at table with statesmen. When he came near me, I longed to speak to him in a lofty fashion. I imagined myself entering into an earnest discussion about the work. How he would point out that every regulation had been properly observed. How I would scourge his complacency! How, instantly, he would recognise me as one of the elect. There was no work on hand at that moment. Boldly, with a beating heart, I took a book, placed it deliberately on the counter with its fluff, its loose threads, its broken staples, and began to read. Shocked, the forewoman whisked the book out of sight and whispered: You want to get me into trouble? I flicked my pony-tail and announced: But it's irrational not to let people read when there's nothing else to do. Meanwhile, with a very slight nod of recognition at the old woman – the baffled look in his sharp eyes of one who reluctantly acknowledges an obligation without ever being willing to repay the debt – the owner passed out of sight.

The fact that I am going somehow leaks into the atmosphere. At night I can hear my father raging to my mother: No girl of mine leaves this house. To my face he presents a stony face. I keep expecting a veto which is never issued. He asks me with an air of great scorn: What's the big idea? In the end, cowardly, swallowing my pride, I intimate that somehow my qualifications are not quite suitable for the home university. I feel unable to assert rights in this matter and slink secretively away. Since there is no quarrel, there can be no reconciliation, and I am left feeling at a disadvantage. To go away is a costly business but I do not feel I can make demands. I am aware that in this respect to have stayed would have been much easier. My mother helps me, scrimping out of the narrow margins of her budget, arranging finally for my trunk to be carried free in a factory van and for me to ride in the cab to save the fare. She keeps telling me how proud he is of me, and I want to be reconciled, but there is no meeting-ground for us except on his terms; and I am determined to go. This little act of rebellion will prevent me for ever from asking for help or from ever admitting a need.

The old man finally died alone in the night. At midday a neighbour that had a key to the house ran crying into the street. By the time we came home from work the remains were cleared away, and exactly one week later a removal van collected the other things, which were not sold but were distributed amongst the few members of his family.

The abortive love affair cannot survive without a point of connection; we live in the same district but it is not possible for us to go openly to each other's houses. Once we meet by accident outside the bread-shop. He seems uncomfortable. I wait for an invitation which is not forthcoming. Decorum makes it out of the question for me to do more than look questioning. I sense that it is not circumstance that has produced the check but a falling away of interest. Within a few moments – the loaf of bread lodged under his arm, his hands in his pockets – he turns away. I say: I shall be going away soon. Relieved, he smiles. He says: Write me a letter sometime. I watch him cross the road. There is an obstinate set to his shoulders. Safely across on the other side, he grins and makes a feint of passing the loaf. Well, he says, it was a good try.

Tongue-tied in his company, I spend my last weeks at home writing innumerable poems in which I inveigh against God for inventing different religions, while at the same time I secretly suspect that we were estranged not so much by bigotry as by his passion for rugby, tennis, and other girls. I sit at the dressing table, staring at my own face in the glass, fearing to face the isolation that follows on the heels of recognition: that he is only the mirror-image of my heart's desire leaves me with a dying cadence, a sense of the sadness of early autumn evenings when the soot from the first fires begins to settle softly on the window-sills. Dissatisfied, I sift through these pages, wanting something more tangible, more achieved. Seeking an appropriate form I achieve only approximate meanings in a language that is often inflated, evasive, off the point. Most remains outside or under the text. Much is hidden from myself. My own body is not present at all. My red-checked gingham dress with its ric-rac braid seems out of place. Moreover, even in my infant system God is already an anachronism, is merely a poeticism that stands for two great strands of thought converging from East and West. To make progress I need a joining. And thus, not long afterwards, I will show these poems to the professor whose kindly face encourages me to confide and – his eyes gently stroking my cheeks – he will tell me very kindly, his clear eyes without a shadow of a doubt, that these outpourings lack every attribute of poetry known to man. Silenced by this setback, violated by the sublime egotism of this judgement, I will spend the best years of my life trying to find my own voice. It will be half a life-time before I learn to look down the long dim corridors of the past, to read these traces, these specks of dust, these hidden leaves, and to listen to the voices of these ghosts. And then, only then, will I begin.

And I shall tell you – for you are there, after all – my reader, my friend, my other self, my reason, my absolute: be resolute; resist; remember above all that you are not alone and because you too are going to die – you and you and you – we owe it to each other to unmake these false gods and to release each other from these perishable bonds.

On a golden October evening I drag my battered trunk over the threshold of the residence in which I have been allocated a place and a porter helps push it into the lift that takes me to the third floor, where my room is a neat box with utility furniture and a wide window overlooking a garden. I put away my clothes and set out my alarm clock, my row of new books and my writing case; and wonder whether it is permitted to pin postcards to these walls. Although the building is full of people and the excitement of fresh arrivals, it is surprisingly quiet in the room, which has the uncanny stillness of a vacant place. My presence is an intrusion, parting the air, which, but a moment ago, had a seamless unity. I feel out of place. I have nothing to do. Nothing compels my attention. Nobody bids me. There are no chores here. This seems strange. I comb my hair for a long time. I make a Grecian knot of curls on the crown of my head, admiring my looks. My face regards me in the glass. How soon will it be before he finds me, the one? After a while I lie on the bed, missing my family, feeling lonely and at a loss. My mother will be frying bacon and perhaps sausages and a tomato or two. She will be thinking of me and wondering, and worrying. And within a few more minutes my father will have rushed out to his evening meeting, while my sister will escape into the street. I imagine that now at last I am free. But I do not know what to do with this supposed freedom. What is freedom after all but a new necessity, a necessity to make choices? I need another person to tell. I go to the desk and take out a new writing pad, which I place on a desk which is otherwise quite empty. What shall I say? I listen intently as the note of panic sounds softly, warningly, like a faint thunder that marks the breaking of a long hot spell. What can I tell?

My letter will be a model of good sense, full of cheerful anecdote. I can never be a disappointment. I gaze down into the garden and begin to scribble: the blond furniture, the white walls, a paved walk between tumbled flower-beds. Proudly, my mother will read aloud at the kitchen table to soothe his concern and so I must show my best face. My success will reward his constancy. Subjected, creature of circumstance, he loves me as his subject, and, grieved by my insurrection, he needs his consolation. But who can I really tell? I need another person. I sit, staring, as the gulf widens between the sunlit evening and the dark centre. Panic. Panic. Is there anybody there? My hands crawl across the shining surface, clutching the friendly pen. My eyes hurry along the paved walk between the herbaceous clumps collapsed by frost. I am a hollow vessel resonating with a high, shrill note. I listen. Along the corridor a gong is sounding and someone is calling: Dinner in half an hour.

Relieved, I dress myself carefully in my best dress. I wear my new blue shoes. I must be prepared. Perhaps I shall bump into him breathlessly on the stair. Perhaps our glancing eyes will meet in a moment of recognition that will transform the universe and I shall see the world with new eyes. Quickly, I slip the letter into the envelope; it is my first letter home. But as I lick the seal – doors slamming, footsteps, voices, hurry, hurry – I suddenly see the skylight, the blue square of air, and myself writing with a stump of pencil on a small piece of lined paper: Grandma says we need some money because my black shoes have fell off my feet. I lick the top of the pencil and spit out a tiny ball of purple spit. I want to tell my mother something very nice to make her feel happy. I tilt back my head, waiting for another seagull. Shall I tell her about the sharp shell, like the shaving blade hanging on a leather thong by the sink in the kitchen down below, where the man soaps and scrapes his skin, chuckling: Come and taste a little bit of chin pie? Or the licking of salty lips when the wind skims the foam into our faces as we battle hand in hand along the promenade while the galloping waves dash for ever and for ever against the wall? After a while, memory comes in a rush and I write: Today I had five black cherries for my tea. The gong sounds again. My eyes fill with tears, but I press down the flap firmly and slip the letter into the pocket of my dress. Now I am really on my own. Gathering myself together, listening for one last moment to the clatter and the chatter before I fly down the stairs, checking my nose for shine, my stocking seams, my smile, brimful with the hope that everything will somehow against all the odds come out right in the end, I stand very still.